DEMONS KNOW MY NAME

A practical guide to elevating your faith
And becoming a serious threat to the enemy.

DEMONS KNOW MY NAME

STEPHEN MCCLELLAN

Cover Design and Interior Formatting
by Michelle Young, Rock Forest Publishing

ISBN: 979-8-9952516-0-6

Demons Know My Name / Stephen McClellan. – 1st ed.

To my son, Carson Bo.
May you one day become the warrior
God created you to be.

"The greatest single cause of atheism in the world today is Christians who acknowledge Jesus with their lips and walk out the door and deny Him by their lifestyle. That is what an unbelieving world simply finds unbelievable."

-Brennan Manning

Table of Contents

AUTHOR'S NOTE

Before We Get Started...

There are a few things I want to mention up front.

First, if you are a high school student and claim to be a Christian, then you need to know I wrote this book specifically for you. Not that these principles won't span outside of that age range, but you're my focus here. The reason is simple: you're in a horrific war against the enemy, and I want to help you win that war.

I've been a teacher for the last fourteen years—middle and high, public and private, nationally and internationally—and I've seen firsthand the influences you face every day. Influences that most adults struggle to fully grasp because they can't fathom facing those challenges at such a young age and in such a toxic cultural climate. Without a doubt, I believe the most significant and critical spiritual battles are being fought in students between the ages of fifteen and eighteen years old. And now more than ever we need you to stand in the midst of those influences and fight for God's heart. That's why this book is for you.

On that note, I say that I wrote the book specifically for students who claim to be Christians because if you're reading this book and you don't believe in God, don't buy into any faith in particular, or in some way have become jaded toward Christianity itself, then the topics discussed here could potentially come across as judgmental or condescending, further entrenching you in your distaste toward organized religion. It could be easy to get defensive and point the finger right back at me (the middle finger at that) and swear off ever showing any interest in Christianity again. That's the last thing I want.

If you profess to be a Christian and claim to have accepted Jesus as your Lord, Savior, and King, then the motto "I can do what I want, when I want, and how I want" no longer applies to your life. Jesus has called us to a higher standard of living, and with a higher standard of living comes a higher level of accountability. This book critiques the way followers of Jesus are living, and if you aren't a follower of Jesus then I have no right to condemn any lifestyle choice you are making. (I don't have a right to condemn anyone at all, but you know what I mean.) I wanted to make sure I covered that up front because it's important to set the context for what you're about to read.

Second, I've read self-help books in the past that seem to be talking *at* you rather than taking the journey *with* you. I want this experience to be different. At no point do I want you to feel like I've got it all together, or that I'm insinuating I've reached a higher moral ground than other people, or that I'm judging those beneath me. Because I don't, I haven't, and I'm most definitely not. I'm no better, and if anything, I've written this book just as much to hold myself accountable as to help you take a stand for your own faith.

Getting completely transparent, I'm tired of not being a threat to the enemy. I'm tired of not being taken seriously because of things I think and say and do. I want to take a stand, and I need your help holding me accountable just as much as you need to be held accountable yourself. So when I say I'm *with* you, I mean it. I hope you feel that in these pages. Remember, the Christian faith is at its strongest when believers form a united front to fight against the enemy. So in that sense, we're all in this *together.*

Finally, I want to make something very clear right out of the gate. This entire process is not about perfection; it's about *progression.* A constant growth, a gradual increase, an upwards trend to becoming more like Jesus. We all slip up. We all lose focus. We all spiral from time to time. It's the essence of being human. But are we satisfied staying there? Are we trying to be a better person than we were the day before? Are we seeking genuine change? Do we recognize areas we need to improve and are showing some type of effort to improve them? Do we even care at all about trying to live a better life? That's what's important.

If you feel convicted, guilty, or even frustrated at your own choices while reading this book, then that's not a bad thing. We all need to be pushed and even called out at times to keep growing and elevating our level of faith. But if you're reading this book and you have an overwhelming sense that you aren't good enough, can never measure up, or simply want to give up your faith journey because you feel like you're fighting a losing battle, then either I didn't do a good job communicating something or maybe you misinterpreted something that you read. I hope that doesn't happen. Perfection is beyond our control. Progression is within our control. And that's what we're going to focus on.

I've waited a long time to take this journey with you. I hope you're ready.

Let's get to it.

INTRODUCTION

The Ultimate Question

I want to tell you a story.

There's this group of guys, right? And they hear about a famous traveling preacher who can heal people and perform miracles and do a bunch of pretty radical stuff—including cast out demons. So they decide to copy his methods and travel around also trying to cast out demons. From the looks of it, they're pretty good. I mean, these guys have all the bells and whistles: they carry the title, they look the part, they say the right things, and they speak with confidence. The only problem? One demon isn't fooled. And it gets nasty, quick.

It's from the book of Acts in the Bible. Check it out…

|11| God gave Paul the power to perform unusual miracles. |12| When handkerchiefs or aprons that had merely touched his skin were placed on sick people,

they were healed of their diseases, and evil spirits were expelled. |13| A group of Jews was traveling from town to town casting out evil spirits. They tried to use the name of the Lord Jesus in their incantation, saying, "I command you in the name of Jesus, whom Paul preaches, to come out!" |14| Seven sons of Sceva, a leading priest, were doing this. |15| But one time when they tried it, the evil spirit replied, "I know Jesus, and I know Paul, but who are you?" |16| Then the man with the evil spirit leaped on them, overpowered them, and attacked them with such violence that they fled from the house, naked and battered. -Acts 19:11-16 (NLT)

One line. That's all it is. One line that establishes the battle lines between good and evil. One line that shows us the amount of preparation it's going to take to engage the enemy and the extent to which we'll have to sacrifice if we want to win this fight for humanity.

"I know Jesus, and I know Paul, but who are you?"

I know Jesus, and I know Paul. Essentially, "I know their reputation. I know who they represent. I know the miracles they've performed. I know the power they carry. I know how they're capable of destroying me."

But who are you? "But I've never heard of you. I don't know where you come from. I'm not familiar with any miracles you've performed. I'm not aware of any power you hold. I'm not convinced you're capable of doing anything that could harm me."

In other words, the demon wasn't fazed. He wasn't filled with fear at the sight of the exorcists, despite knowing what they had come there to attempt.

You think he would have at least been somewhat intimidated, but he didn't sense any danger. He didn't feel threatened. And here's the reason why: *even demons recognize a hypocrite when they see one.*

Which leads us to the central question, the central premise, of this entire book. If we know that demons can tell whether or not you're the real deal, whether or not you're bringing the smoke, then the ultimate question boils down to this: "Are you a serious threat to the enemy?"

Meaning: Do Satan and his demons take you seriously, or are you an afterthought? Does it invoke fear in them when you step out of bed in the morning, or do they laugh at your feeble attempts to rebuke them? Has your reputation preceded you and been passed down through the enemy ranks as someone who isn't afraid to claw and scratch and bite and bleed in battle? Do they quiver at the knowledge you possess, knowing you draw your power from the One who can't be defeated? *Does the enemy even know your name?*

The reality is that simply carrying the title of "Christian" won't protect us. It's not enough to look the part or say the right things or speak as if we know what we're talking about. Because the enemy isn't fooled. The devil has trained his army to be smarter than that, to detect the ones who are a serious threat compared to the ones who can't even lace up the straps of their spiritual boots. Satan knows the ones who can be taken down by a single arrow as well as the ones who will require him to call in his reinforcements. If the enemy sees your house swaying in the wind because the foundation is made of Jello, then you can scream threats at him on your porch all you want, but he'll still belly laugh at you and proceed to demolish your home.

So what does this mean for us?

It means the time has come to rise up and take back the territory the devil prematurely claimed when he thought we hadn't amounted to anything. The territory he claimed while we were going through that phase, or stuck in that cycle, or lost in that habit, or defeated by that temporary mindset. The time has come to join the fight. The real fight. Not the one where we hang out in the back because we're too afraid our breastplate will get scratched or that our shield will be stained with blood, but the one taking place on the front lines where we stand firm and stare Satan and his demons in the face and watch as their smiles fade.

The time has come to live spiritually lethal.

This book is a declaration that we will no longer be a warrior who the demons fail to recognize. That we will no longer be lost in the shadows, adrift, lifeless, and nameless. That we will no longer self-sabotage and allow the enemy to feast on the scraps. The days of lukewarm and in-between and one-foot-in-one-foot-out Christianity are over. We will be a relentless force that decides and declares once and for all, "I am a soldier in the army of Jesus Christ, the one true King, and demons know my name."

PART 1

Threat Level

CHAPTER 1

Room Raiders

So exactly how big of a threat are you to the enemy? There's a way to find out.

If you want to know if the enemy takes you seriously, then you first need to ask yourself if you take the battle seriously. What does "taking the battle seriously" mean? It means taking your relationship with Jesus seriously. And how do you know if you're taking your relationship with Jesus seriously? That's what Part 1 of this book is all about.

We're going to analyze four different categories in Part 1 to help determine our "threat level." In this chapter, we'll discuss the first piece, *physical evidence*, and in Chapter 2 we'll look at the other three pieces: *spiritual motive, measure of sacrifice*, and *level of persecution*.

First things first…

PHYSICAL EVIDENCE

When I was in high school, a popular show aired on MTV called *Room Raiders*. (All my early 2000's teens know what's up!) It was a reality dating show where three contestants would be "kidnapped" from home and driven around town while their rooms were "raided" by another contestant of the opposite sex. The raider would do a deep dive into all three rooms—sort through sock drawers, look under the bed, check out the closet, comb over the place with a black light, observe what's in the nightstand, etc.—to try and get an idea of each contestant's interests, habits, and overall personality.

After all three rooms had been raided, then the raider would choose one person to take out on a date based on their findings. All pictures of the contestants had been removed from the rooms, so the raider had to make their decision strictly from what he/she found in the room. An impression, based on an appearance, provided by evidence.

As I thought about the premise of the show, a memory popped into my mind from when I was younger. I'm not sure where I was or who I was with when I heard it, but I remember being challenged with the question, "If you were accused of being a Christian, would there be enough evidence to convict you?" Thinking back on it, the question seemed a bit elementary by nature at first (most likely because I tied it to my childhood), but the more I pondered it the more I realized it was the perfect place to start when analyzing our threat level.

There's something to be said for finding physical evidence that following Jesus is a priority to us.

So let's take a second to ask ourselves this question: If you were accused of being a Christian and an unspecified team was assigned to investigate every aspect of your life, would there be enough evidence to conclude that you are a sold-out, committed follower of Jesus Christ? I'll fire off a few questions to get you reflecting on this idea as well as some possible answers that will either affirm you or gut-punch you.

Consider with me…

~If the team walked through your room, what kind of vibe would they get concerning the decor on the wall or the atmosphere you had created?

Would there be any sign of spirituality, positive thinking, and inspiration, or would the room be littered with inappropriate images and signs of unhealthy obsessions?

~If the team turned on your tv and logged into your streaming accounts, what movies or shows would they find on your recently watched list?

Would there be wholesome shows that foster a positive mindset and lifestyle, or would your lists be filled with shows that contain nudity, sex, inappropriate language, and toxic themes?

~If the team accessed your music accounts, what songs or bands would they find on your playlists?

Would there be at least some semblance of maturity and appropriateness, or would there be songs with explicit language that promote immoral lifestyles and behaviors?

~If the team skimmed through your library of books and video games, what would they find lining the shelves?

Would there be books that help you grow in your personal life and that have innocent narratives with healthy plot lines (maybe a Bible on the shelf), or would your collection contain books with sexual content and ungodly themes? Would there be video games that are innocent in nature while still engaging and fun, or would there be games that promote pornographic material, drugs, and other unhealthy narratives?

~If the team raided your desk drawers or your secret hiding place for personal items, what would they find stashed there?

Would there be items for daily living—perhaps even items with significant or nostalgic memories attached to them—or would there be items found like drugs, alcohol, or even things your parents have banned you from owning?

~If the team logged onto your computer and went through your search history, what websites would they find you had last visited?

Would there be innocent sites such as sports, shopping, education, or random Google searches, or would the history show inappropriate sites that will only bring temptation and destruction?

~If the team combed through your social media profiles, what impression would they get from the information in your bio, the people you followed, the posts you made, the comments you left, the pictures you liked, the videos you shared, and the accounts you last searched?

Would they find healthy content that promotes hope and encouragement, a supportive community, and a respectful online presence, or would they find vulgar language in your captions and comments, posts that don't honor yourself as an individual, and you idolizing people who are terrible influences in today's society?

~If the team scanned through your text messaging conversations (and had access to the deleted ones), what content would they find?

Would there be fun, positive, healthy, innocent conversations with family and friends, or would the messages be filled with gossip, drama, bullying, sexting, and pictures you'd be mortified for your family and closest mentors to see?

~If the team wiretapped your phone or placed a hidden microphone on you, what types of conversations would they overhear?

Would they hear uplifting, encouraging, mature, and spiritually-driven conversations, or would they hear you curse every other word, spill the tea about everyone, and constantly dwell on subjects that don't foster a healthy mindset?

~If the team accessed your purchasing history, in what areas would they find you spending most of your money?

Would it be on responsible items you want or need that are innocent by nature, or would it be wasted on things that serve no real purpose and foster destructive mindsets, habits, and addictions?

~If the team had access to observing you in your house, in your car, on your bus, in your school, or at your job, what might they conclude about how you spend your time, the habits you've formed, and the lifestyle you maintain?

Would they find you engaging in a healthy lifestyle with habits that will benefit you physically, mentally, and spiritually, or would they find you wasting your time, developing toxic habits, pursuing an insignificant lifestyle, and no sign of spirituality in your daily routines?

~If the team monitored your involvement in church activities, what would they find concerning your participation?

Would they see you volunteering, actively engaging in worship services, participating in small groups, and fostering community, or would they find you simply going through the motions, more concerned with your phone than the sermon, and only going to church events because it's "what everyone is doing" or because that one hot guy or girl will be there (or perhaps never stepping foot through the doors at all)?

~If the team examined your friend groups, who would they find that you invest most of your time, energy, and emotion in?

Would you be with friends who have your best interests at heart and pour into your life in a positive way, or would the team find you surrounding yourself with people who bring destruction, temptation, and toxicity?

~If the team observed the relationship with the person you're dating, what would they see?

Would they see a relationship with healthy boundaries where you hold each other accountable, improve each other's lives, and help each other grow closer to Jesus, or would they see a relationship centered around sexual activities, selfish motives, and constant arguing?

~Finally, if the team interviewed your family, friends, neighbors, co-workers, classmates, teachers, and anyone else affiliated with you, what would those people testify about you?

Would they genuinely celebrate you, have nothing but positive things to say, and uphold your integrity, or would they struggle to find encouraging things to say about you because of the negative way you conduct yourself and treat those around you?

SO WHAT DO YOU THINK?

After the search had been conducted, do you think the team would conclude you were actively pursuing Jesus, or would they move on to the next case because there wasn't enough evidence to convict you? Remember, this isn't an exercise of "how good is good enough" or trying to look perfect; it's simply to foster the awareness of how serious we take our relationship with Jesus. Like I mentioned at the start of the chapter, if you're taking your relationship with Jesus seriously, then likewise, you're taking the battle against the enemy seriously.

This list might seem superficial (even judgmental to a degree), but let's talk about that. If our tendency is to immediately get defensive or angry and start to rationalize or debate each topic, then most likely that's a sign that there is some pride in our life concerning how we want to or think we should be able to live. Don't take my word for it. Just read in the Bible at what Jesus has to say about how we should act concerning the thoughts we think, the words we speak, the habits we form, the health of our body, the people we surround ourselves with, the way we treat sexuality, and the manner in which we pursue righteous living in general (to name a few).

Jesus is the one who calls us to a more abundant life. It's the enemy who says to do what you want, how you want, when you want. So if we're willing to argue over how we believe we should be held accountable and what we have the "right" to do, then it's probably a sign there are still sinful areas or desires we are holding onto a little too tightly.

If we don't overcomplicate it and look at it from a common-sense perspective, then as the old saying goes, "The proof's in the pudding." Think about it. Jesus' influence should infiltrate every area of our life.

If there is little to no sign of Him in the rhythms of our daily lifestyle, then chances are there is little to no effort being put into actively pursuing Him. You may think it's not that simple, but it is. Satan recognizes it, and you should too. Satan knows the level of priority you place on pursuing Jesus is the level of priority he needs to place on pursuing you. If Jesus is a big deal to you, then your threat is a big deal to Satan.

It's not hyper-spiritual or legalistic or "old school" Bible-thumping-thinking; it's the basic truth that our focus produces our fruit. If we focus on negative influences and invest our time in activities that produce nothing of value, then our fruit will be worm-eaten and rotten. Whereas if we focus on positive influences and invest our time in activities that produce things of quality, then our fruit will be ripe and abundant.

What is the first way to evaluate if you're a serious threat to the enemy? Analyze whether or not you are intentionally pursuing an active, growing relationship with Jesus that permeates throughout each area of your life. If you are, then your threat level is high. If you're not, the enemy is probably rolling his eyes at you.

CHAPTER 1 - DISCUSSION GUIDE

Chapter Recap:

If you want to know if the enemy takes you seriously, then you first need to ask yourself if you take the battle seriously. There's something to be said for finding physical evidence that following Jesus is a priority to us. If there is little to no sign of Him in the rhythms of our daily lifestyle, then chances are there is little to no effort being put into actively pursuing Him.

Discussion Questions:

1. Do you think having physical evidence in your life that you are a Christian really represents your relationship with Jesus? Where do you agree or disagree?

2. Likewise, how do you find a healthy balance of maintaining the right perspective in this area rather than allowing yourself to obsess over it and potentially lead you to become legalistic in your lifestyle?

3. Respond to the question, "If you were accused of being a Christian, would there be enough evidence to convict you?" Choose the category where you might find the least amount of evidence of Jesus in your life, and talk through why you think you might struggle in that area.

Action Step:

Take the category where you feel you have the least amount of evidence that you follow Jesus, and choose one practical step you can take to make a change in that area this week.

CHAPTER 2

Three Pieces

"**B**ut hold up. Isn't it petty to strictly base someone's spiritual pursuit on appearances alone? After all, even the Bible says that people pay attention to physical appearances, but God looks at your heart. There are so many other factors that really prove whether or not you are a follower of Jesus."

I hear you. Which is why these next three categories are equally important. Let's talk about them one at a time.

SPIRITUAL MOTIVE

Your motive is simply the real reason behind why you do something.

I'm not naive to the fact that people can live a spiritual lifestyle without actually being spiritual. There are people who can put a healthy checkmark by every example listed in Chapter 1—from the shows they watch, to the clothes they wear, to the friends they have—yet still be missing what the Christian life is all about.

Maybe some of you know someone like that—someone who outwardly has it all together. They have a great reputation, parents love them and want you to be friends with them, they make spiritual social media posts, they're active in FCA, they attend small groups or Bible studies, they sing in the church's worship band, and on and on. But behind the scenes? Well, they're not as cookie-cutter as they appear. You've heard things they've said, you've seen ways they've acted, and you know what they're really into. There are other reasons behind why they act the way they act and talk the way they talk, and it *isn't* because they are all about Jesus. There's always an ulterior motive for why they do what they do.

What can ulterior motives look like?

> *~You go to youth group every week but only because you have a crush on a person that also goes.*
> *~You sign up to play or sing in the church band but only because it will earn you more clout.*
> *~You volunteer to lead FCA but only because you like being the center of attention.*

~You put Bible verses in your locker but only because you want people to think you're a good person.

~You make spiritual social media posts but only because it makes you look like a deep thinker.

~You go to church every Sunday but only because you're worried what people will think about your reputation if you don't go.

~You go on mission trips and participate in service projects but only because it will look good on college applications.

~You wear hoodies with spiritual messages but only because it's the current trend.

~You attend every youth event but only because everyone else is doing it.

~You help people when they really need it but only because you know they'll owe you one if you ever need help.

I don't know what you've seen, and obviously this list doesn't cover every example, but you get what we're going for here. Your motives have to match your movements. If not, then there will be a disconnect between you and God that will put a dent in your threat level.

This is why having the right motive is so important. Having a pure heart was really important to Jesus, so it needs to be really important to us. If you don't believe me, think about how Jesus responded to the religious leaders who only cared about their appearances but had insincere motives? He blasted them in front of everybody, calling them a bunch of snakes and hypocrites (Matthew 23). I think He was serious about doing things for the right reasons.

Think about your current spiritual lifestyle and why you make the choices you make. Do you make them strictly for appearances: to gain popularity, to establish a certain reputation, to get in good with a certain crowd, or to earn a particular position? Or do you make them because you genuinely want to be more like Jesus, be faithful with what He's given you, and become the person God created you to be?

That may seem like I'm oversimplifying it, but it's really that straightforward. The position of your heart determines the purpose of your hands. What you repeatedly do flows from who you are at your core.

Now, I do want to throw something else out there. Notice, I used the words "but only because" in the examples above. I'm not saying you can't have other things that also interest you about a decision. There might be multiple reasons you choose to do something, and not all of those will be bad. But if your *only* reason for pursuing something spiritual is based off a selfish or prideful motive, then something needs to change. I just wanted to make sure we're clear on that.

One last thing to note is that if you pursue Jesus with a pure heart, then you won't need to "put on appearances." The evidence from your lifestyle will naturally overflow into every aspect of your life mentioned in Chapter 1. I remember my dad saying one time, "Take care of your character and your reputation will speak for itself." If you make decisions from a righteous motive, God will help align your desires, mindset, and habits to produce fruit that honors Him. In that way, His presence will be obvious in your life.

What is the second way to evaluate if you're a serious threat to the enemy? Analyze whether or not you have a genuine, spirit-led motive that guides your decision-making. If you don't, then Satan will be able to sniff out the counterfeit on you like a drug dog on illegal cargo. Like we referenced in the introduction, the enemy isn't fooled by people putting on an act. He's smarter than that.

MEASURE OF SACRIFICE

There are a lot of descriptions used to define commitment, but one of the most significant definitions in my opinion is that *commitment requires sacrifice.* If you want an honest look at how deeply a person is committed to someone else, then take an honest measurement of how much they're willing to sacrifice for that person.

How does this apply to what we're talking about? Well, does following Jesus require you to give up anything? Or another way to put it might be to ask, "Does following Jesus inconvenience you at all?" Do you ever have to sacrifice your time, your energy, or your resources? How about your pride or your pain? Sometimes sacrificing for Jesus doesn't mean literally giving up your life (though sometimes it does); it means recognizing that the cause of Christ is greater than the cause of self, and you're willing to do something about it.

What can making sacrifices look like?

~When you get up a few minutes early to read your Bible before school, you're sacrificing sleep.

~When you dress modestly rather than posting inappropriate outfits that will gain you followers, likes, and shares, you're sacrificing attention.

~When you comfort your friend who just called needing your support rather than turning on the latest episode of your favorite tv show, you're sacrificing entertainment.

~When you choose to let go of a past that's beyond your control rather than holding onto your anger, you're sacrificing bitterness.

~When you spend a Saturday afternoon serving at a local ministry rather than hanging out with friends, you're sacrificing time.

~When you don't seek revenge on a friend who betrayed you, you're sacrificing pride.

~When you quit hanging out with a particular friend because you know that person is a terrible influence on you, you're sacrificing friendship.

~When you use your allowance to support a local ministry rather than spending it on the new pair of shoes you wanted to buy, you're sacrificing desire.

~When you don't go to a party with your friends because you know there will be a lot of temptation to participate in unhealthy things, you're sacrificing pleasure.

~When you take a stand for Jesus even when your opinion is mocked by everyone around you, you're sacrificing popularity.

Every sacrifice—small or large, significant or seemingly insignificant—represents a measure of commitment you have for someone or something. When the enemy sees you sacrificing the things that matter the most to you just so you can be a little more like Jesus, it automatically strikes fear in him. Why? Because when you show devotion to anyone other than Satan, he can feel himself slowly losing the grip he has on you. It automatically forces him to take you more seriously because he will see you're not as superficial as he originally assumed.

What is the third way to evaluate if you're a serious threat to the enemy? Analyze the extent to which you're willing to sacrifice for Jesus. The enemy hates when you do it, and that's why we must insist on it.

LEVEL OF PERSECUTION

Backlash from the enemy:

Satan doesn't like it when we pursue our faith. In fact, he can't stand it. He loathes it. It's the water to his witch, the sunlight to his vampire, the Voldemort to his Harry Potter, the heaven to his hell. Satan wants all of you so he can destroy all of you, and as long as you remain faithful to Jesus and not to him then he doesn't have full control over what he's trying to destroy. And what do people do when they sense they are losing control? They get desperate. They're willing to do anything to turn you back, to change your mind, and to convince you otherwise.

I think it's no coincidence that when you finally start getting your life in order and begin pursuing healthy habits and mindsets again that things can start to crumble around you. Old temptations raise their heads. Past hurts creep back in. Long-lost regrets resurface. One wave hits, then another, and another. As the saying goes, "When it rains, it pours." Can we chalk every bad thing that happens up to the devil and his schemes? Certainly not. But would he do anything to keep you bitter, battered, and blinded? Absolutely.

I believe there is a level of persecution the enemy tries to rain down on those who choose to follow Jesus. Stress, frustration, anger, bitterness, confusion, and disappointment all have ways of driving a wedge into our faith and our endurance, and I'm convinced it's why Satan tries to utilize pain in any way he can. He knows that if he can cause enough hurt and discomfort in our lives, then there's a possibility we will turn our back on God and retreat further into darkness. It's one of his biggest plays, and it's yet another reason why we must be rooted in what we believe.

This may be bold of me, but I've always thought that if you're not sure about the whole God thing and want to know if He's real, then simply leave your old lifestyle and see what kind of persecution you face. An army doesn't like losing its soldiers to the other side, and the prince of darkness will do anything to preserve his ranks. If you suddenly encounter a lot of personal problems—whether physical, emotional, or psychological—it might just be a sign that you're on the right track, and there's someone who isn't happy about it.

Backlash from other people:

When Jesus called people to follow Him, He didn't say it was the cool thing, the popular thing, the entertaining thing, or even the fun thing. He said the opposite, actually. Jesus warned his disciples that they would be beaten, imprisoned, and hated by everyone (Matthew 10:16-23). And He was telling the truth. When it was all said and done, ten of His twelve disciples would be martyred for their faith (with the eleventh being banished to live out his remaining days on a deserted island and the twelfth hanging himself from the guilt of betraying Jesus).

I'm not saying you will be killed because you believe in Jesus (although this does happen around the world, whether we hear about it or not), but you need to know that you will definitely receive some backlash from other people for following Jesus and standing by your Christian convictions.

What can backlash from other people look like?

> *~You stop getting invited to certain group hangouts because those people don't think you're willing to have "fun."*
>
> *~You get canceled on social media for taking a stance that doesn't fit cultural agendas and isn't deemed as popular.*

~Your classmates alienate you from their group because you refuse to cheat on the homework and tests like everyone else.

~Your best friend drops your friendship because you don't want to follow him/her down the corrupt path they're headed.

~You begin getting bullied in school because you defended someone who was being treated horribly.

~Your boyfriend/girlfriend breaks up with you because you won't go farther physically with them than the boundaries you put in place for yourself.

~You get laughed at and mocked by your friends because you don't want to take a drink, or watch an inappropriate movie, or sneak out of the house when you're not allowed.

~You get labeled as a "snitch" because you did what you felt was right and talked to an authority figure about a sensitive issue that needed to be addressed.

~You aren't considered "popular" because you would rather maintain your integrity than gain attention through ways that compromise your convictions.

~You get accused of being judgmental and hateful because you choose to stand by your morals and values rather than adopting someone else's "truth" as your own.

When we get down to the bare bones, we must ask ourselves if we have ever received some form of persecution—harassed, treated cruelly, or treated unfairly—for following Jesus. If we have zero percent of persecution going on in our lives right now, then we really have to question if we are being proactive in representing our faith, if we're confidently standing by our convictions, and if our faith is driving us outside our comfort zone to actively share Jesus with others. If we're doing these things, then I promise, there will be backlash.

I'm not saying you need to go looking for trouble or start instigating arguments in the name of Christianity. And I'm not saying you aren't a real Christian if you aren't being persecuted in some way. I'm just saying the Christian Walk can seem easy, comforting, and convenient when you remain inside the safety of your own bubble. But people with the highest threat levels don't seek out ease, comfort, and convenience. They live as spiritual giants who aren't afraid to kick the dust up—not because of how loud they can yell but because of how deep they can love.

What is the last way to evaluate if you're a serious threat to the enemy? Measure the level of persecution you have received (or are currently receiving) for living out your faith.

It may help you detect just how angry you've made the enemy. And that should make you smile.

CHAPTER 2 – DISCUSSION GUIDE

Chapter Recap:

Beyond the physical evidence of Jesus in our daily lives, three other ways to evaluate if you're a serious threat to the enemy are to analyze 1) whether or not you have a genuine, Spirit-led motive that guides your decision-making, 2) the extent to which you're willing to sacrifice for Jesus, and 3) the level of persecution you have received or are currently receiving for living out your faith.

Discussion Questions:

1. Is there an area you have not had a pure motive for pursuing your faith? Why do you think that area in particular is so difficult for you to maintain the right motive?

2. What is one area you feel like you do well and one area you feel like you don't do well when it comes to sacrificing something to grow in your relationship with Jesus?

3. Is there an area you feel like you have been persecuted for following Jesus? If so, has it discouraged you from growing closer to Jesus or encouraged you to pursue Him deeper?

Action Step:

Choose one thing you would like to improve concerning what you sacrifice for Jesus, and commit to making a change in that area this week.

CHAPTER 3

Why Does It Matter?

I don't know how you felt after reading the first two chapters—called out or confirmed, offended or at ease—but you may be asking why all of this even matters. Who cares if we're next-level Christians? Who cares if we dabble in this or participate in that? It's not that big of a deal. As long as we've accepted Jesus and know where we're going when we die, then it's all good, right? Why does it really matter if we're a threat to the enemy? There are several reasons, but let's focus on two major ones.

Reason #1

The first reason is that when we fail to be a serious threat to the enemy we are settling for less than we were created to become. There's a quote by C.S. Lewis that really hits home with this idea. In his book, *The Weight of Glory*, Lewis says, "It would seem that our Lord finds our desires not too strong, but too weak. We are half-hearted creatures, fooling about with drink and sex and ambition when infinite joy is offered us, like an ignorant child who wants to go on making mud pies in a slum because he cannot imagine what is meant by the offer of a holiday at the sea. We are far too easily pleased."

We've been created with talents, passions, and potential that go far beyond anything we could imagine. When we choose to settle, to be so easily pleased by the fascinations of the world, it diminishes the potential of our purpose. We miss out on who we were created to be and the impact we were created to have. Our gifts aren't fully utilized, and our influence isn't completely maximized.

I can't help but think how often I've fallen into the trap of allowing the temporary pleasures of this world to monopolize my thinking and distract me from what really matters. Too often I've allowed myself to be so easily pleased by insignificant things when God is sitting there saying, *"but there's so much more beyond those things."* God wants us to see that we are infinitely more than we choose to settle for. And I don't know about you, but I'm tired of settling for mud pies when there's a holiday at sea waiting.

When I was in high school, the band Switchfoot came out with one of their biggest hits titled "Meant to Live." Check out some of these lyrics:

Fumbling his confidence
And wondering why the world has passed him by.
Hoping that he's bet for more than arguments
And failed attempts to fly, fly.

Chorus:
We were meant to live for so much more.
Have we lost ourselves?
Somewhere we live inside.
Somewhere we live inside.
We were meant to live for so much more.
Have we lost ourselves?
Somewhere we live inside.

Dreaming about providence,
And whether mice or men have second tries.
Maybe we've been living with our eyes half open.
Maybe we're bent and broken, broken.

(Chorus)

We want more than this world's got to offer.
We want more than this world's got to offer.
We want more than the wars of our fathers,
And everything inside screams for second life, yeah.

We were meant to live for so much more.
Have we lost ourselves?

The "so much more" and our threat level are intertwined. When we choose to step into the "so much more" and refuse to settle for less than our value holds, our threat level is maximized. We really were meant to live for so much more, and living as a threat to the enemy is a sign that we are stepping into what God intended for our lives all along.

Reason #2

There's a second reason why it matters that we're a threat to the enemy, and it has to do with a little trip I took to the beach.

One summer back in college, I went with my brother and a few friends down to Panama City Beach, Florida to spend a week on vacation. The hotel we were staying at didn't have a lot going for it, but it did have a hot tub, and that hot tub was the place to be when every evening rolled around.

A couple nights into our stay, our group was down there hanging out. There were girls. There were drinks. Everyone was introducing themselves and saying where they were from and what they'd been doing. I was in the middle of the mix enjoying myself when I started talking to a guy beside me.

I was just shooting the breeze—beer in my hand, arms propped up on the sides of the hot tub—when he took an interest in the tattoo I have on my right shoulder. It's the first tattoo I ever got, and it's a tribal image of Jesus wearing the crown of thorns with the scripture reference John 8:32 on either side of it. I can't remember the exact setup of the conversation (I think he had asked about the tattoo, and I was explaining its significance), but I'll never forget his response to me. He said, "Sooo, you have a tattoo of Jesus…and you're drinking a beer." I kind of shrugged and quickly replied, "Yup" (because what else can you say).

I'm writing this nearly 16 years later, and I can still remember how awkward I felt. And I know some people might think it was a judgmental or legalistic comment and that just because I have a tattoo of Jesus doesn't mean I can't drink a beer. (That's an entirely different conversation in itself.) But honestly, when I look back at that interaction, none of those thoughts occur to me. I'm not offended, and I don't get defensive. Because I get what he was saying.

I think his comment was more than just, "If you have a tattoo of Jesus, then you can't drink a beer." It was as if he saw the contradiction between Jesus and the world.

He was talking to someone who was claiming to follow Jesus, quoting a verse about how the truth would set you free. It was clear that the guy in the hot tub knew enough about religion to associate it with maintaining healthy habits and surrounding yourself with positive influences.

Meanwhile, he looks around at the environment we are in, and what does he see? A party scene, guys and girls flirting, some people on their way to getting drunk while others are already there, groups heading out to the club passing by groups returning from the club, and me sitting by in the midst of it all, drinking my beer, *actively participating.*

I remember the vibe I got from him, the look on his face, and you could see he was thrown off, slightly confused, like it didn't quite make sense. It was clear that in his mind the principles I claimed to stand for didn't line up with the activities I was participating in. There was a disconnect somewhere. This entire interaction illustrates the second reason why it matters so much that we are a threat to the enemy: hypocrisy hurts the cause of Christ.

The world is watching. It is looking for and *desperate* to believe in something real and genuine. When we claim to believe in something but then act hypocritical toward it, not only does it discredit those beliefs, but it also repels the people we are trying to convince to believe in them as well. We see it every day. In our culture, we call out frauds and roll our eyes at people who claim one thing but then act on another. It's laughable, unreliable, and *un*believable. And it's an immediate turn off to whatever is being introduced.

We can't profess Jesus in public but then run back to the addictions we keep in private. We can't talk about God in front of our class but then treat people like dirt outside of class.

We can't write a caption about how important God is to us in one post but then flip off the camera and dance to filthy song lyrics in the next post. We can't put Bible verses in our social media bios but then post pictures showing more skin than clothes and sexualizing our bodies. We can't mentor others on how to act but then turn around and deliberately ignore those principles in our own lives. It just doesn't work that way.

In the Bible, John bluntly puts it, *"If someone claims, 'I know God,' but doesn't obey God's commandments, that person is a liar and is not living in the truth. But those who obey God's word truly show how completely they love him. That is how we know we are living in him. Those who say they live in God should live their lives as Jesus did"* (1 John 2:4-6, NLT).

CHAPTER 3 - DISCUSSION GUIDE

Chapter Recap:

The first reason it matters that we are a serious threat to the enemy is that when we fail to be a serious threat to the enemy we are settling for less than we were created to become. When we choose to be so easily pleased by the fascinations of the world, it diminishes the potential of our purpose. God wants us to see that we are infinitely more than we choose to settle for.

The second reason it matters that we are a serious threat to the enemy is that living a hypocritical lifestyle hurts the cause of Christ. When we claim to believe in something but then act hypocritical toward it, not only does it discredit those beliefs, but it also repels the people we are trying to convince to believe in the beliefs as well. As Christians, our way of life should be uncommon. We must be carriers of light, not barriers.

Discussion Questions:

1. Concerning C.S. Lewis' quote, "We are far too easily pleased," do you think there is an area of sin in your life that you give into too easily? How do you think your life would elevate and improve if you finally got that area under control?

2. How have you seen hypocrisy hurt the cause of Christ in your own life (whether it's something you did or something you saw someone else do)?

3. Is there one area of your life that you think separates you from the rest of the world in a positive way? Why do you think this has been an area of strength for you?

Action Step:

Choose one area you feel like you have helped the cause of Christ and one area you feel like you have hurt the cause of Christ. Pray over both of these areas. Where you have helped the cause of Christ, ask God to continue to give you wisdom, discernment, vision, focus, endurance, and strength. Where you have hurt the cause of Christ, ask God for forgiveness and pray that He gives you perspective, awareness, courage, and the desire to form the discipline to not return to that particular area of weakness.

CHAPTER 4

95-5 Living

To piggyback on what we just talked about in the last chapter, I want to talk about the idea of "95-5."

One of the most obvious signs to tell if you're showing flashes of a hypocritical lifestyle is a concept I call "95-5 living." It means you offer God 95% of life but intentionally withhold the other 5% for yourself. You're willing to sacrifice *almost* everything, but you shove a little bit in your back pocket for safe keeping. It's the line of thinking that goes, "I'm not *that* bad," "I'm *basically* living for Him," "I'm *technically* not sinning," or "I'm *fine* compared to other people." And it's such an easy trap to fall into because when we're doing most things right, it makes the things we still need to improve look like not that big of a deal.

What can 95–5 living look like? You live 95% of your life with positive habits, solid integrity, genuine motives, healthy relationships, and an active pursuit of righteousness, but there is that *one* area you leave unchecked. Such as…

~Your 5% is you maintain a habit of cursing around your best friends.

~Your 5% is you consistently have sex with the person you're dating.

~Your 5% is you selfishly only care about your own problems.

~Your 5% is you constantly talk bad about people behind their backs.

~Your 5% is you get drunk with your friends every weekend.

~Your 5% is you have a secret addiction to pornography.

~Your 5% is you consistently disrespect authority figures.

~Your 5% is you love unhealthy entertainment (explicit music, inappropriate movies/shows).

~Your 5% is you obsess over your image and constantly seek validation from people rather than God.

~Your 5% is you have a problem lying to people.

Or if we're getting really transparent, here's an example from my own life…

Years ago, I went down to Atlanta to go out with a couple of friends one Saturday night. We were out late, and I drank too much. I ended up getting tossed out of the club and getting sick and having a meltdown back at the house. It wasn't pretty. But you better believe when the next morning rolled around that I was showered up, fixed up, and walking into church on time for the service. Walking into Sunday as if Saturday hadn't happened. It was all good.

Except it wasn't.

At that time in my life, I'd say I was a good person. I consistently prayed and read my Bible, I loved my family and friends fiercely, I helped out people who needed help, and I genuinely tried to make the most of every day.

But there were also a lot of times where I loved a good night of drinking too much, which led to some horrible decision-making, embarrassing moments, and damaged relationships. I knew getting drunk was wrong for many reasons, but I often still chose to drink anyway because it was fun, entertaining, and made a lot of memories. *That's* 95-5 living.

Draw up any list you want and chalk it full of stereotypical examples of "doing everything right," but if you are holding back, compartmentalizing Jesus, or placing God in a box, then your heart is not exactly in the right place. Too many people choose their lifestyle first and then wrap Jesus around it where He's convenient and comfortable. It has to be the other way around. You have to choose Jesus *first*, then conform your lifestyle to live as He said to live. As long as one area is off kilter, your life won't be completely aligned and balanced as it should be.

Now, just to be clear, if you have an area where you struggle but you're aware of it, taking action to do something about it, and praying through it every day to surrender it to God, then I would say you are not living 95-5. But if there is a mindset, a habit, or a lifestyle that you have developed that goes against how Jesus said to live and you *don't* see an issue with it, you are *not* concerned about it, or you are actively choosing to *continue* to embrace it, then that's where there is a problem. That's when you know there is 5% that needs to be fixed.

THE LIES WE TELL OURSELVES

I think it's important to mention that one reason we stay in 95-5 living is often because of the lies we convince ourselves are true—cultural norms that we've allowed to become our spiritual standard. Sometimes we don't even realize we've fallen into the lie. The messages have become so ingrained in our thinking that the line between what the Bible says is healthy for us versus what the world says is healthy for us has essentially been erased. It's all one big blur that we will literally fight over and argue with and debate until the sun sets.

Do any of these sound familiar?

> ~*"It's trending, so it's not a big deal. Everyone is posting it."*
>
> ~*"Even if the song curses, it's fine as long as I don't say the words."*
>
> ~*"It's their job to maintain self-control, so I can wear what I want and act how I want."*
>
> ~*"Times are different. This is just what kids do these days."*
>
> ~*"I don't listen to the lyrics. I just like the song for the beat."*
>
> ~*"This is nothing compared to how bad some people act."*
>
> ~*"It's fine to have sex with the person as long as you love each other."*
>
> ~*"Even if it's against the law, it's fine as long as no one gets caught and no one gets hurt."*
>
> ~*"I can say whatever I want. I'm not being mean; I'm just being honest."*
>
> ~*"I'm not addicted. I can stop any time I want."*

I promise I'm not trying to pick a fight here, but these are things we hear all the time in the teaching world.

And while we could go back and forth and hash out why they aren't "technically" wrong, the reality is that the Bible would say otherwise concerning how we're supposed to think, speak, and act. There's simply a healthier way that Jesus wants us to buy into.

I think there are things we deep down would admit we know to be wrong, while other times I think we are genuinely blinded by the lie and don't see what's right in front of us. One time, I saw some students post a TikTok dancing to a song that had some pretty explicit lyrics in it. The ironic part? They were making the video in the lobby of their church. The point isn't that we can act inappropriately as long as we're not in church; it's representative of the fact that sometimes we genuinely don't see how conflicting the lifestyles are that we live. And we have to wake up to it.

Pray and ask God to convict your heart in order to show you things that you consider true but that don't line up with the way the Bible says to live. There might even be ones you're thinking about right now that you're battling through because your first instinct is to defend them. Ask God to give you His perspective on them so you can see them through His eyes, not your own. When you shine light in every corner, the shadows have nowhere to hide.

A FEW LAST THINGS TO NOTE

I want to mention something really quick as we get ready to finish this part of the book. As I was writing these last couple of chapters, a thought hit me: "When you think about what's at stake for living for Jesus, it can put a lot of pressure on Christians. And feeling an enormous weight on your back or feeling pressured into living right could just repel us further from the Gospel because it seems too overwhelming." I want to speak to that for a second.

In life in general, I think a certain amount of "pressure" or "weight of responsibility" is necessary to help motivate us to grow as an individual. It's healthy because it keeps us from growing stagnant, complacent, and frankly, lazy in our habits. And the Christian life is no different. We *should* feel a level of pressure concerning the expectation of how Jesus has called us to live. We can't run from that.

The key is to make sure we are keeping the right perspective of the pressure. When we feel the weight of too much pressure, usually it's because either we have set unhealthy and unrealistic expectations for ourselves, or we are trying to live up to unhealthy and unrealistic expectations someone else has placed on us. And we just can't drown in that. We can't carry the weight of convincing people to believe in Jesus. It's God who changes people's hearts, not us. We can't let that be an excuse to live however we want, but we also can't lose ourselves to thinking our efforts alone will save the world.

So there's definitely a balance we have to find between what's within our control and what's beyond our control. And it's why I think we need to focus on the follow-up actions. We can't control how the world believes, but we can control the effort we put into pointing the world toward Jesus.

We can't control every thought or judgement someone has about us when we mess up, but we can control the responsibility we take for our actions. We may lose our cool, but are we apologizing? We may hurt feelings, but are we making it right? Doing the best we can to grow closer to Jesus and then focusing on the follow-up when we miss the mark are both ways we maintain the right perspective of pressure.

Circling back to what I mentioned in the author's note, we are not talking about perfection, but we *are* talking about progression. When we aim for perfection, we're left frustrated. When we aim for progression, we're left motivated. The Christian walk isn't about living without mistakes; it's about living within grace. We can't forget that.

TYING IT ALL TOGETHER

The enemy's time is running out. He knows this. And since his time is valuable, he's going to be intentional about who he targets. Who poses the greater threat to draw others away from Jesus? People who are already lost in sin and don't resemble Jesus at all, or people who look just enough like Jesus to convince others they are Christians but then act hypocritically to the very principles they profess to live by?

This is one reason many people can't stand Christians and don't take Christianity seriously. It's why Satan utilizes people on the fringe who have one foot in and one foot out of living authentically. He knows he's much more likely to bring down other people through this tactic. Which means as long we continue to be lukewarm in our faith, Satan will use it any way he can to harm the cause of Christ.

You can try a lot of things, including wearing t-shirts that say, "F*** Satan" (which I saw one person wearing; a person very outspoken about their faith, mind you), but as long as a part of your lifestyle is counterproductive to the faith you profess, the enemy will use you like his own personal puppet to do his bidding. There's a mission on hand that is far bigger than us with eternal consequences at stake. And we are called to give every bit of ourselves to join the fight.

CHAPTER 4 - DISCUSSION GUIDE
Chapter Recap:

Jesus wants all of us, not just 95%. If you are holding back, compartmentalizing Jesus, or placing God in a box, then your heart is not exactly in the right place. One reason we stay in 95-5 living is often because of the lies we convince ourselves are true—cultural norms that we've allowed to become our spiritual standard.

Too many people choose their lifestyle first and then wrap Jesus around it where He's convenient and comfortable. It has to be the other way around. You have to choose Jesus *first*, then conform your lifestyle to live as He said to live. It's not about perfection, but it *is* about progression.

Discussion Questions:

1. Why do you think we hold on so tightly to our "5%" areas, and why are they so difficult to surrender to Jesus?

2. Is there a lie you have told yourself, allowed yourself to buy into, or convinced yourself to believe about why it's okay to do something that doesn't honor Jesus? What was the thought process that slowly wrapped you up into that lie?

3. Do you think people have unfair or unrealistic expectations of Christians? Likewise, have you ever personally felt the "pressure" or "weight of responsibility" that comes with being called to live like Jesus? How did you handle it?

Action Step:

Think of a "5%" area you need to change in order to grow closer to Jesus. (It may be something similar to the areas you wrote down for Chapters 1-3. If so, that's fine.) Choose one change to make in that area, and commit to praying victory over it every morning before you start your day this week. If you want to take it a step further, talk to someone you trust about the area you want to improve and ask that person to help hold you accountable as well.

PART 2

The Battleground:

Influences

CHAPTER 5

Demon Reconnaissance

Let me tell you where we're headed.

Part 1 was all about how to analyze your life to see if you are a serious threat to the enemy and why your threat level matters. Here in Part 2 we are going to focus on Satan's strategy for trying to threaten you and the areas you as teenagers are the most susceptible to be attacked in today's culture. This will set the stage for Parts 3-5 of the book where we will dive into practical strategies on how you can intentionally maximize your threat level to fight against the enemy.

So on to Part 2.

In order to know how to be a serious threat to Satan, you first need to do some demon reconnaissance work to better understand his personal tactics. In this chapter, we are going back to the first account of where the war started between Satan and mankind. The moment where Satan revealed his true colors and the battle lines were drawn in the sand (or in this case, a tree). In this story, we'll get a good picture of who Satan is at his core and the main strategy he uses to attack us.

Time to do a little reconnaissance work.

SCOUTING OUT THE ENEMY

The story takes place in Genesis chapter 3, and it's one you are most likely very familiar with:

> |1| Now the serpent was the most cunning of all the wild animals that the Lord God had made. He said to the woman, "Did God really say, 'You can't eat from any tree in the garden'?" |2| The woman said to the serpent, "We may eat the fruit from the trees in the garden. |3| But about the fruit of the tree in the middle of the garden, God said, 'You must not eat it or touch it, or you will die.'" |4| "No! You will not die," the serpent said to the woman. |5| "In fact, God knows that when you eat it your eyes will be opened and you will be like God, knowing good and evil." |6| Then the woman saw that the tree was good for food and delightful to look at, and that it was desirable for obtaining wisdom. So she took some of its fruit and ate

it; she also gave some to her husband, who was with her, and he ate it. -Genesis 3:1-6 (HCSB)

Who is Satan?

You can tell a lot about Satan's character by analyzing what he tries to accomplish.

First, Satan tries to plant a seed of doubt in Eve's mind by questioning God's instructions: *He said to the woman, "Did God really say, 'You can't eat from any tree in the garden'?"* (v 1). It says Satan was the craftiest of any beast that had been created, so we can assume he already knew Adam and Eve were not supposed to eat from *every* tree of the garden. But by questioning what God had told her, perhaps Satan could get Eve to reevaluate the command, creating even the tiniest fissure in her thinking.

Second, Satan stirs up confusion by directly opposing God's consequences, essentially calling God a liar: *"No! You will not die," the serpent said to the woman* (v 4). The scriptures don't directly state it, but I imagine it was one of the first times Eve had ever heard a creature blatantly disagree with and defy the Creator of the universe. It was something she certainly wasn't accustomed to hearing or had encountered before, which surely added a heightened sense of confusion.

Third, Satan tries to manipulate Eve's thinking by introducing an alternative explanation as to why she shouldn't eat the fruit: *"In fact, God knows that when you eat it your eyes will be opened and you will be like God, knowing good and evil"* (v 5). By proposing this idea, Satan was really calling into question God's motive of why He gave Adam and Eve the command in the first place. Obviously, the verses don't tell us everything Eve was thinking, but it's easy to see how it could have planted a seed of curiosity in her mind that made her start questioning things she had never questioned before. Questions like: "Is this true?" "Has God been lying to me?" "Is God withholding something from me?" "What else is out there that I don't know about?" "What was God's real intention for creating me?" "Could I really gain that type of wisdom?" "Could I really be like God?"

To summarize, what did Satan try to accomplish? He tried to create doubt by forming a crack in her reasoning, foster confusion by destabilizing a foundation she once thought stable, and manipulate her thinking by introducing a new explanation as to why God said what He said. Doubt, confusion, manipulation, all meshing together to form one giant deception. Or as John 8:44 says, *"He has always hated the truth, because there is no truth in him. When he lies, it is consistent with his character; for he is a liar and the father of lies"* (NLT).

So who is Satan at his core? He is the father of lies, and everything he does is rooted in deception.

What is his main strategy?

What notion started Eve's mental downward spiral that ultimately led her to sinning? Her desire. *"In fact, God knows that when you eat it your eyes will be opened and you will be like God, knowing good and evil." Then the woman saw that the tree was good for food and delightful to look at, and that it was desirable for obtaining wisdom. So she took some of its fruit and ate it; she also gave some to her husband, who was with her, and he ate it* (v 5-6).

There were already plenty of trees with fruit for food in the garden. There was already beauty surrounding her. She already had a source of wisdom in God Himself. She had everything she needed. But in that moment, those things weren't enough. In that moment, being *Eve* wasn't enough. She desired more, and that desire led her to sin.

I think there's truth to the idea that the root of every sin is pride. Pride is choosing what we want, when we want, and how we want, apart from God's best for us. In its most basic form, pride is when we obey us rather than obeying God. If we're talking about sin itself, obviously pride will be at the center. But Satan doesn't make us sin; he tempts us to sin. So if we're talking about the main strategy he uses to tempt us to sin, I think it's the way he tries to influence our *desires*.

At our core, what are some of the things we all naturally desire? Fun, entertainment, adrenaline, popularity, acceptance, affirmation, pleasure, joy, justice, affection, love, peace, comfort, convenience, courage, fulfillment, purpose (and so much more). The key isn't that we desire those things; it's what we do to *satisfy* those desires. Satan knows if he can entice us to satisfy our desires through the world rather than through God, then it will not only lead us to sin but also to our ultimate destruction.

Desiring wisdom isn't a bad thing in itself, so the Tree of Knowledge of Good and Evil wasn't bad in itself. But God had commanded them not to eat the fruit. It wasn't that Eve wanted to be smarter; it was that she was willing to sin against God in order to gain that wisdom. It was gaining knowledge apart from God. *That* was the problem. As the book of James tells us, *"Temptation comes from our own desires, which entice us and drag us away. These desires give birth to sinful actions. And when sin is allowed to grow, it gives birth to death"* (James 1:14-15, NLT).

So what is Satan's main strategy for attacking us? He tries to influence our desires so we care more about satisfying ourselves than we do about serving our Savior.

SO WHAT DO WE DO WITH THIS?

I think there are areas Satan uses to target you specifically because he knows what influences impact the desires of your life right now. The influences that capture our attention will be the factors that determine our direction, and in high school, I believe there are three areas of influence in particular that capture our attention the most: *relationships, social standing, and pop culture.*

In the following chapters, we're going to break down each of these areas one at a time to hopefully make us more aware of how Satan uses them to influence our desires, why it's so easy to fall victim to his schemes, and practical strategies we can use to help us make wiser choices.

CHAPTER 5 - DISCUSSION GUIDE

Chapter Recap:

Who is Satan at his core? He is the father of lies, and everything he does is rooted in deception. What is his main strategy for attacking us? He tries to influence our desires so we care more about satisfying ourselves than we do about serving our Savior. What are three of the most powerful areas of influence that Satan will use to try to shape our desires? Our relationships, our social standing, and pop culture.

Discussion Questions:

1. In what ways do you believe Satan tries to manipulate us in today's society?

2. Was there a time when the enemy tried to sabotage your thinking and it made you question something about God? How did you navigate through that situation?

3. In what areas do you think Satan has tried to morph your desires personally? Why do you think he has targeted those specific areas?

Action Step:

As you prepare to read the next three chapters of this book, take a few minutes to pray that God would reveal to you which desires have had the most control over you. Ask God to reveal His truth through these chapters about those desires, to help you detect Satan's lies within them, to give you courage as you face them, and to give you victory as you withstand their temptations moving forward.

CHAPTER 6

Relationships

Years ago, I was offered a position at a middle school to create an alternative classroom for students with behavior issues. Essentially, if students committed zero-tolerance offenses (like bringing weapons or drugs to school) or their behaviors were so bad that they couldn't function in the regular classroom, then they were removed from their entire schedule and placed in my room full-time.

I had an assistant with me, and it was our job to establish a program to teach the students their core subjects, help them fix their behavior problems and develop healthy habits, and gradually integrate them back into the regular classroom. By the time students landed in my classroom, usually they had already faced a number of disciplinary measures, were already in the court system, and had been in and out of juvenile detention. Needless to say, we saw some pretty rough behaviors.

One day, we received a new girl to the program. I was walking her down the hall, getting to know her a little bit, and introducing the procedures of our classroom. When I opened the door to my room, I nodded to a few students and asked her if she knew anyone. She scanned the room and immediately pointed to three different kids. "That's my cousin right there…that's my best friend sitting there…and that boy over there is my ex-boyfriend."

You've all probably heard the principle, "You become like the people you surround yourself with." And I agree with it, although I would add in one small change: You become like the people you *consistently* surround yourself with. Was it any surprise, then, that this girl, her cousin, her best friend, and her ex-boyfriend all just happened to end up in the same behavior class? Absolutely not. It was a perfect example of how our relationships (whether positive or negative) influence our choices, which in turn influences who we become.

I want to narrow this topic down a little further though.

When I taught leadership development classes, I did quite a few reflective journal entries and activities with my students. In one activity in particular, I asked the question, "Who is the one person you value the most?" I assumed the most popular answer would be the students' parents or mentors (and that did happen), but it was surprising how often the students answered with either their best friend or their boyfriend/girlfriend.

The more I thought about it, the less surprised I should have been. We tend to listen to and be impacted by the people we invest the most trust, time, and emotion into. If you're a teenager, the people who fall into those categories are most likely your inner circle of friends and the person you are dating.

A relationship with someone technically means the connection you have to that person, whether that's a friend, family member, teacher, pastor, mentor, boss, or stranger. But in this chapter, when I say "relationships" I want to focus on these two specific groups: your closest friends and who you date.

It's said that our friend circle starts small in elementary school, expands through middle school, peaks in high school or college, and then begins to decrease and minimize again as we grow older. Which means for the phase most of you are in right now, your social life is a big deal. Likewise, it's why so many teenagers find "quality time" as their current love language.

You don't need me to tell you this, but our relationships have huge potential to influence our desires and decision-making. Think about all the different areas our best friends and our crushes can impact us on a daily basis: our mood, our thought process, our attention, our conversations, our habits, our time commitments, our relationships with our family, our financial purchases, our stance on politics, our perspective on life, our *view of God*. We focus the most on who we care about the most, so if we care about our closest friends and the person we are developing feelings for, then that is where most of our focus will be placed.

It might be obvious to you, but why would Satan target our relationships? At our core, we all seek acceptance, validation, and love, which are all established in some form through the relationships we keep in our lives. If Satan can work at manipulating our relationships, then he can work at morphing our desires. When it's all said and done, Satan targets this area because he knows the health of our relationships often dictates the health of our spirituality. So the real question is, how do we be wiser concerning who we surround ourselves with and who we date? Let's break down those two categories to try and approach them in a practical way.

CHOOSING YOUR FRIENDS

I get that this is a huge topic with a million different approaches you could take, but I'm going to try to take a simple one: a Bible story and a few questions for application.

|1| When Jesus returned to Capernaum several days later, the news spread quickly that he was back home. |2| Soon the house where he was staying was so packed with visitors that there was no more room, even outside the door. While he was preaching God's word to them, |3| four men arrived carrying a paralyzed man on a mat. |4| They couldn't bring him to Jesus because of the crowd, so they dug a hole through the roof above his head. Then they lowered the man on his mat, right down in front of Jesus. |5| Seeing their faith, Jesus said to the paralyzed man, "My child, your sins are forgiven." |10| Then Jesus turned to the paralyzed man and said, |11| "Stand up, pick up your mat, and go home!" |12| And the man jumped up, grabbed his mat, and walked out through the stunned onlookers. They were all amazed and praised God, exclaiming, "We've never seen anything like this before!" - Mark 2:1-5, 10b-12 (NLT)

We're going to use this story to analyze the type of friendships we have and the type of friendships we should be investing in. Take a second to reflect on these next three questions.

Three Questions

1) Do you have friends who carry you when you can't walk?

The friends in the story literally carried the paralyzed man when he couldn't walk. They supported him in his darkest, most discouraging moments. On a very basic level, we need friends in our lives who will empathize with us, encourage us when we are feeling defeated, walk beside us through trials and challenging experiences, and support us when life is hard. Do you have friends who show up in moments like that in your life?

2) Do you have friends who support your hopes and dreams?

Even though the Bible doesn't tell us these things directly, I would imagine that the paralyzed man's biggest dream, his lifelong desire, was simply to be able to walk. When his friends heard there was a man who could possibly heal their friend and make his dream come true, they didn't roll their eyes, ignore their friend's desire, or abandon him to find another way. They showed up, and they carried him directly to Jesus.

Just like we need friends who show up for us in the discouraging times, we also need friends who support us in the encouraging times. We need friends who empower us to reach our hopes, dreams, and ambitions; friends who will help us reach our potential, accomplish our goals, and be genuinely happy to see us succeed.

3) Do you have friends who will do whatever it takes to get you to the feet of Jesus?

A lot of us can check #1 and #2 off the list, but #3 can be a challenge. It's by far the most important piece. When his friends couldn't get the paralyzed man through the front door, they didn't give up, shrug, and take him back home. They tore the house apart. They risked owing everyone an apology for the damage done or people they offended. They were willing to even sacrifice their own reputation. All for what? To get their friend to the feet of Jesus.

Bluntly put, we need friends who push us closer to Jesus, not pull us farther away. We need friends who will be a good influence, instill positive mindsets and habits, care about our spiritual health, and encourage us to continue to grow as a follower of Jesus. We need friends who will pray for us, fight our battles alongside us, hold us accountable, show us grace, and do whatever it takes to help point us back to Jesus. Even if a sheep is considered weak, if it's surrounded by a pack of lions protecting it then other animals won't try to attack it.

Test yourself. Do you ever feel like you're the only positive influence or voice of reason in your friend circle? Do you feel like you're the one who is constantly having to keep everyone out of trouble? Do you get made fun of because you won't participate in certain activities? Do you feel like you're always investing into people, but no one ever really invests into you? Maybe it's time for a change in friend scenery.

For The Ones Questioning...

If this is the case, some of you may be asking, "How do I do that? I can't just randomly drop my friends and quit hanging out with them."

That's fair, and here are my thoughts on it. You don't technically have to make things awkward and drop them all at once. Simply start living like Jesus said to live. That's it. Then sit back and watch. The ones who are on board and want the same things you do will stick around and elevate with you, while the rest will naturally fall off and quit hanging out with you on their own. I promise, you don't have to walk away from them. If you live like you should be living, then the ones who aren't ready for that or don't want that accountability in their lives will walk away on their own.

You might also say, "They are my only friends. If I quit hanging out with them, then I literally will have no one else." This is a more difficult one to address, but you have to ask yourself if you'd rather have company in the dark or temporarily walk alone in the light. Jesus recognizes when we're trying to surround ourselves with the right people, and I think He rewards us for that. I truly believe that if He sees you removing yourself from negativity and toxic influences, then it's only a matter of time until He brings the right kind of people into your life. You may temporarily feel alone, but He won't leave you there. Plus, the light you emit will naturally attract like-minded people who want to be around you and will be healthy for you.

It may seem like I'm oversimplify it, but I don't think we have to complicate things to know who is healthy to keep in our life. You need friends who will encourage you when life is hard, empower you when life is good, and always push you to grow closer to Jesus. Friendships fuel our desires, and we can choose whether those influences are healthy or unhealthy, whether they lead to life or lead to death.

I have just one final thought to bring this home, and it's one of the most important to consider. When the paralyzed man was brought before Jesus, a miracle was performed in his life. But it never would have happened if he hadn't invested in the right people who were willing to help make it happen. And I can't help but think, maybe Jesus wants to work a miracle in your life, but He is waiting for you to surround yourself with people who will help put you in a position for Him to work that miracle. Maybe He needs you in a certain position or place in your life before He fully reveals Himself, and the only way to get you there is by investing in the right people who will help that become a reality for you.

It may not be a physical miracle. It may be a mental or emotional or spiritual one, or maybe one that happens in a way you least suspect it. But I know that when we get to the feet of Jesus, miracles happen. And the people we surround ourselves with determine how quickly we reach the feet of our Savior.

CHOOSING WHO YOU DATE

There have been so many times students have talked to me about either a person they are interested in or a person who is interested in them, and students will make comments to me like, "I don't know whether I like him or not," "I don't know if I should date him or not," or "I kind of like her, but I just don't know what to do." Some will straight up ask me, "So what should I do? Go out with this person or not?" So much uncertainty, so much confusion.

I want to offer a few thoughts that I think can help with this. Usually, when you are considering who to date, you focus on the other person. But I want to give you five things I think *you* need to do personally before you jump into a relationship. They are ones you probably have heard before, but they are all extremely important.

1. **You need to know who you are as a person before you decide who you need to date.**

    It just makes sense—how do you expect to know what you need if you don't know who you are. We will cover this in Parts 3 and 4 of the book, so we won't dive into it too much right now. But concerning this first piece of advice for dating, you need to evaluate your identity and purpose and then find someone who values your worth in those areas.

2. **Once you have a better understanding of who you are as a person, you need to create a list of core values and qualities you are looking for in the person you date.**

    This is a really important point, so let's talk about it for a minute.

    If I were you, I would have two categories: a list of core qualities and a list of bonus items. Core qualities are the qualities you know you definitely want (and need) in the other person, the "must haves," or the "non-negotiables." The bonus items are the areas that aren't "make or break" for you but are considered a bonus if the person does possess them. Core qualities will typically be character or lifestyle-driven, whereas bonus items will be interest or hobby-driven. (For example, a core quality might be the person loves Jesus, whereas a bonus item might be the person likes sports.)

So if you could choose your ideal person to date, what are the most important qualities you would want that person to possess? Someone who actively pursues their faith, will lead you spiritually, or has a heart for overseas ministry? Someone who is hard-working or health-conscious? Someone who you can laugh or cry with? Maybe it's important to you that someone is adventurous and spontaneous, is musically inclined or bilingual, or takes initiative and has an entrepreneurial spirit?

There are so many important qualities out there—respectful, responsible, kind, gracious, loyal, empathetic, humble, positive, patient, encouraging, disciplined, determined, etc.—and it's up to you to decide what you want as well as what you need. Whatever the areas are, I would be as specific and concise as possible.

As an example, here is my own list of core qualities and bonus items I wanted in my future wife that I wrote back in 2014:

Core Qualities:
-Pursues God daily

-Humble (has a servant's heart)

-Has a heart for missions and overseas ministries

-Challenges me to grow in my faith and holds me accountable

-Trustworthy (loyal and honest)

-Has a positive outlook on life and a good sense of humor

-Supports my hopes and dreams

-Spontaneous and fun

-Good communicator

-Goal-driven

Bonus Items:
-Likes college football

-Listens to country music

-Physically beautiful

I think it's important to create a mature list of qualities—not because you're seeking perfection or setting unrealistic expectations for someone—but because you're being intentional about the type of person you know is healthy for you, will protect your heart, will be a positive influence in your life, and will ultimately value your worth as an individual. If you develop a list and try to stick to it, then not only will it save you loads of heartache, frustration, and regret, but it will also put a preventative measure in place to protect you against people Satan will try to use to infiltrate your life in unhealthy ways.

If you have no standard, then anything goes. Or as a speaker I heard back in college say, "Stand for something, or fall for anything." When you don't have a standard, you're essentially waiting for the other person to tell you who you should be interested in or the type of person you need to date. Who you go out with each time is more of an experiment to see how it works out rather than an intentional choice of who you think is healthy for your life. When you don't have a standard, you settle for less than your worth. You are subconsciously morphing your interests and personality to fit the other person's agenda rather than evaluating whether or not that person should even be a part of *your* story.

(Suggestion: Once you've made a list for yourself, run it by a person or couple you trust who is in a healthy marriage and follows Jesus. Sometimes qualities we think are important or qualities we desire as high schoolers may be somewhat jaded to what Jesus says is best for us. Having wise people pour into your life and go over your list with you will help clarify that the qualities you've listed are genuinely a mature way of thinking.)

Now, for three more pieces of advice.

THREE MORE PIECES OF ADVICE

1. **If you expect to date a person with amazing qualities, you first have to possess those qualities yourself.**

If you want to find the right person to date, then create a list of standards for yourself. But if you want to be *datable*, then you need to become those standards. Often, we want people to possess certain qualities, but if we're honest, we don't care to or don't want to go to the trouble of possessing those same qualities in our own lives. You might find the person you've been looking for, but if you don't possess those same qualities, then that person may not see you as the person *they've* been looking for.

A person who loves Jesus won't typically pursue someone who never reads their Bible. A person who cares about fitness won't typically pursue someone who sits on the couch all day and never exercises. A person who values hard work typically won't pursue someone who is extremely lazy. It just makes sense. Whatever type of person you're looking for will most likely be looking for a similar type of person in many ways. And if you are the polar opposite (in the areas that matter, the core qualities), then you can't expect to ever date that person. Keep that in mind.

2. **Just like people say you need to know your "why" for pursuing a goal, the same goes for pursuing a person.**

Motive matters. You have to make sure you're pursuing someone for the right reasons. On their end, if you are *just* pursuing someone because the person is popular, attractive, talented, or rich, then that isn't healthy.

On your end, if you are *just* pursuing someone because you are bored, afraid, insecure, or lonely, then those aren't healthy reasons either. I inserted the word "just" to mean that if you are pursuing someone for one of those qualities alone, then it isn't healthy. Now, if you are pursuing someone for the right reasons and they happen to be popular, attractive, talented, or rich as well, then that's different. Similar to making your list, a person's core qualities should come first and their bonus items second.

If you want to test yourself, then simply ask yourself the question, "Why are you interested in this person?" Usually, the first thought that enters your mind is the driving force behind why you want to pursue that person. Know your "why," and make sure it's a healthy one that will draw you closer to Jesus.

3.   Finally, be patient before you commit.

If you hurry and commit to someone because you are afraid the person may not like you anymore if you don't date them within a few days, then that person isn't for you. If they genuinely like you and are serious about pursuing a relationship, then they will still feel that way a week, two weeks, or a month later. Don't let your emotions make a premature decision. There is wisdom in waiting.

To tie everything together, I heard a speaker one day comment that we are made up of the top five most important relationships in our lives. Essentially, he said to show him your five most valued relationships that you invest in, and he'd show you your future. As we close out this chapter, I don't want you to just pass this up. Take some time to evaluate the people you consider your closest friends as well as the people you typically date. The relationships you maintain are some of the biggest areas that impact your life right now, and you have to make sure you are surrounding yourself with positive influences. Satan is intentional in the way he weaves together toxic relationships, so we have to be intentional in the way we weave together healthy relationships. Let's win that battle.

CHAPTER 6 - DISCUSSION GUIDE

Chapter Recap:

We tend to listen to and be impacted by the people we invest the most trust, time, and emotion into. If you're a teenager, the people who fall into those categories are most likely your inner circle of friends and the person you are dating.

Concerning friendships, you need friends who will encourage you when life is hard, empower you when life is good, and always push you to grow closer to Jesus. Concerning who you date, you need to do these five things: know who you are as a person, create a list of core values you want in the person you date, make sure you possess those core values yourself, know your "why" for pursuing the person, and be patient before you commit.

Discussion Questions:

1. List specific examples of how your friends have influenced you (positive as well as negative).

2. If someone had never met you personally, what qualities would they say you possess strictly based off the qualities of your closest friends and/or the person you are dating?

3. If you had to choose three things that you use to determine who to date (looks, personality, spiritual life, etc.), what would they be? Why are those things important to you?

Action Step:

Create your own "Dating List" of core qualities and bonus items that you would ideally want in the person you date. Once you are done, share your list with a mentor and discuss it together.

CHAPTER 7

Social Standing

Closely linked to the relationships we maintain is the social standing we uphold. It's naturally ingrained in all of us to want to feel seen and heard, to feel like we belong and are important in some capacity. Even if your personality is more chill or introverted, you still seek acceptance and the awareness that you matter to someone. And in our culture today, what is one thing that boosts our ego, self-worth, and overall feeling of importance? It's our social standing.

We live in a world that measures your purpose according to your popularity and interchanges your identity with your image. It leaves us with the pressure to perform, as if we need to accumulate likes, shares, views, followers, and subscribers online in order to feel validated. As if we need to know the right people and get connected with the right group to be highlighted. That who we are is defined by what we do, and what we do is only as credible as the social standing it elevates us to.

Why would Satan target our desire to have a good social standing? We often allow our image and popularity to define our identity and purpose. Satan knows if he can taint those areas, then it can do serious damage in influencing the way we view our own existence as well as the existence of God. When we desire being seen over being sanctified and having followers over having freedom, then Satan's already got us right where he wants us.

So let's spend a few minutes talking about this.

HOW FAR ARE YOU WILLING TO GO?

Two main components that make up our social standing are our image and our reputation, and these two things are linked. One is what we portray to people, and the other is how people interpret that portrayal. And we need to make sure we are on the healthy side of both things.

I don't think wanting a good image, wanting a good reputation, wanting people to like you, and even caring what people think of you are bad desires in themselves. Do I think it's important to do your best to establish a good reputation? Absolutely. Do I think there are times you should care about your image? I do. If you didn't care at least a little bit about your image, you would probably not be prepared for the job interview, not make a good impression with your teachers, not make any friends, and not take care of yourself concerning your hygiene (to name a few). But when does it go too far?

I think the danger we get into is not that we care about those things; it's what we are willing to do to *gain* those things. How far are we willing to go to have a good reputation? To make sure we are noticed, accepted, validated, or feel a sense of belonging? What are we willing to sacrifice to make sure people think we're cool and pretty and popular? Think about how far you've seen people willing to go and some of the things you've seen people willing to do in order to portray a certain image or establish a certain reputation.

For example, I've seen people…

~disrespect authority figures, pull stunts, or act out

~dress in a provocative or attention-seeking style

~break the law

~develop unhealthy lifestyles to maintain a physical appearance

~cheat on tests

~bully others

~compromise their integrity on social media to gain followers

~be willing to send sexual pictures and messages
~betray their friends and gossip about others
~hang out with people who are unhealthy influences

Or how about…

The shoes mess your feet up, but you wear them strictly because they look good. You can't sit down because your shorts are too short, but you love the way your butt looks in them. Staying out past curfew will get you in trouble with your parents, but you don't want to come across as uncool by ending the night early. Drinking or vaping isn't healthy for you, but you don't want to spoil the mood by rejecting their offer.

What are you willing to sacrifice? Your comfortability, your health, your safety, your dignity? Your relationship with your family or friends? Your relationship with *God?* How far are you willing to go? What are you willing to do?

All of these examples don't come close to covering everything, but you get the point. Whether the acts are ultimately harmless or harmful, every day you ride the bus, walk the halls, sit in the classroom, or go to work with people who try extremely hard to establish their social standing in some form or fashion. Sometimes it's obvious, and other times it's not so obvious. But even as you read this, I'm sure someone's name has popped into your mind (even if it's your own).

So how do you address this? Where's the line between caring too much about your image and reputation (social standing) and not caring enough? How do you determine what is a healthy desire compared to what is an unhealthy desire? Let me give you a simple way to evaluate.

EVALUATING YOURSELF

As the saying goes, this isn't easy, but it's simple. If you want to evaluate yourself, then before you do anything, you should ask yourself one question: *what's my motive?*

Why do I want to wear this outfit? Why am I spending so long getting ready? Why do I want to make this post? Why do I want that job? Why do I want to take that class? Why do I want to sign up for that club? Why do I want to attend that event? Why do I want to date that person? Underneath it all, if you're completely honest with yourself, what's the *real* reason you are making the decision?

We talked a little about motive in Chapter 2 and then again in the last chapter, and I want to circle back to a few of those points. If you make the decision because it honors God, aligns with who He created you to be, further develops your passions and potential, or brings you a healthy level of happiness and fulfillment, then I would say your motive is good. But if you make the decision to feed an obsession, insecurity, or satisfaction not rooted in God, then your motive is not so good.

I think it's worth noting that if you make a decision for healthy motives and it naturally improves part of your social standing—your image, reputation, or popularity—then great. But those things need to be a byproduct of your motive, not the motive itself. It's not necessarily wrong to want to feel popular or pretty or cool, but when those things become the root for how you make all your choices—from online to in person—then you have to be careful.

Because there is so much more *beyond* these things. Beyond people's opinions of us and their expectations for us; beyond our darkest fears and deepest insecurities; beyond the pressure to conform and fit in; beyond shallow popularity and misplaced admiration; beyond the boundaries we have created for ourselves. We must begin to live *beyond* those things.

I know we haven't talked about it, but one minor note that's not really a minor note at all is the comparison trap. Sometimes our motives are rooted in how we compare ourselves to others. It's human nature to compare ourselves at times, even if we're not consciously aware that we are doing it. And you better believe Satan will try to morph your desires by getting you to look outward.

That's why we can't lose sight of the simple fact that comparison and peace don't hunt together. God didn't compare you to other people when He was choosing how to design you, so it only makes sense that comparing yourself to other people won't satisfy you. It's literally not in your DNA. So if you find yourself not at peace with your image or reputation, analyze your motive to see if you've been comparing yourself in different ways. If you can get that under control, I promise you'll find peace in your purpose rather than pressure from your comparisons.

Let your motives be rooted in who God says you are and who He created you to be (which we'll talk about later in the book). When we take our eyes off of God and look to the world for fulfillment, Satan springs the trap. Again, the enemy knows your social standing can heavily influence your desires, so don't fall prey to the things he flippantly tosses at you. You're worth more than that.

CHAPTER 7 - DISCUSSION GUIDE

Chapter Recap:

Two main components that make up our social standing are our image and our reputation. The danger we get into is not that we care about those things; it's what we are willing to do, how far we are willing to go, and what we are willing to sacrifice to *gain* those things.

Where's the line between caring too much about your social standing (image and reputation) and not caring enough? If you want to evaluate yourself, then before you do anything, you should ask yourself one question: *what's my motive?*

Discussion Questions:

1. Do you think you care too much about your image or reputation? Why or why not?

2. Building off of what we discussed above, where do you personally think the line is between caring too much about your image and reputation and not caring about them enough? List specific examples.

3. In a world that is image-obsessed and popularity-driven, what is one way you think we can be intentional about maintaining the right motive when it comes to how we approach our image and reputation?

Action Step:

Think about things you've done to try and establish your image or reputation, and analyze the areas where you haven't had the right motives spiritually. Pray and ask God to give you the clarity of how to change those motives as well as the courage to walk in truth, victory, and freedom.

CHAPTER 8

Pop Culture

Out of the three categories of influences mentioned here in Part 2, I'd say the impact pop culture has on us is the most extensive. Tv, movies, music, social media, literature, videos games, sports and other areas of the pop culture scene are often major obsessions (and therefore play a major role in influencing our spiritual life).

We impersonate who we idolize and adhere to who we admire. We listen to songs on repeat and learn the dances that become trends. We binge watch streaming apps when the next season of that series is released and constantly have tv shows, movies, or music playing in the background any time we are in our room. We get fashion tips, makeup tutorials, and life hacks from all social media platforms. Pop culture's influence seeps through almost every area of our life, whether we care to admit it or not.

Listen to some of these statistics. At the time of writing this, soccer icon Cristiano Ronaldo has 671 million followers on Instagram. Actor and singer Selena Gomez has 415 million. The song "Despacito" by Luis Fonsi (ft. Daddy Yankee) has over 8.9 billion views on YouTube.

The Super Bowl in 2026 had an estimated 127 million viewers, making it the largest audience to watch a Superbowl as well as a single-network telecast in TV history.[1] As of 2023, it's estimated that the *Harry Potter* series has sold over 600 million copies, making it the best-selling book series of all time.[2] As of late 2025, there is an estimated 5.4 billion social media users worldwide, which is approximately 65% of the world's population. Facebook and Instagram both have 3 billion users, followed by YouTube with 2.5 billion, TikTok with 1.6 billion, and Snapchat with 932 million.[3]

All of these statistics are difficult to grasp if you stop to think about them. I'm not saying there's something wrong with having social media or watching sporting events or listening to music, but it does show that we place a lot of focus on them.

Why would Satan target our interest in pop culture? We tend to be the most easily influenced by the things we find the most entertaining. We are hard-wired to be passionate about things, and when we are passionate about something then we're easily susceptible to the influence it has over us—be it a sport, an actor, a musician, a streaming service, or a social media app. So we must constantly be aware of how much time, energy, and emotion we are placing in our fascination with pop culture as well as the influences we are allowing our minds to soak up. Satan will prey *on* them, so we must pray *over* them.

There are tons of different strategies we could discuss to help us be wise in our approach to pop culture, but obviously we don't have time to talk about them all. Instead, I've chosen three basic rules I think can make a pretty big difference when it comes to how we allow pop culture to influence us.

Check these out.

1. Create boundaries

Guardrails are set up to help keep your car from running off the road and hurting yourself or other people. Boundaries do the same thing in our lives. They are put in place to help prevent us from veering off the path and potentially causing damage to ourselves or the people we catch in our wake. Have you set up a boundary on what you allow yourself to watch, listen to, or read? Most people haven't even thought about it, and it's one reason we so easily slip into unhealthy patterns. It takes intentionality to pursue positive influences in these areas.

I get that setting up boundaries can be tricky. A few years ago, I was having a discussion with my 8th grade students about how pop culture influences us. I asked if anyone had created boundaries for themselves concerning different outlets of media. One kid raised his hand and said, "I look up a movie beforehand, and if it has over 200 f-words in it then I don't watch it." I loved that he had at least considered a boundary to put into place, although even some of his classmates started laughing and gave him a hard time because they thought he was allowing himself a little too much wiggle room there. Some of y'all would agree, while others of you might think the boundary was a pretty fair one.

I know we're all different, and what may be a temptation for some may not be a temptation for others. That means we need to be wiser and pray that much more about the boundaries we put into place. If you're not sure how to gauge it, I would say two rules of thumb to follow are to 1) base your boundaries off of what the Bible says is healthy for your life, and 2) evaluate the areas of temptation in your life where you are the most easily susceptible, and put up boundaries in those areas.

2. Choose positive role models

We obviously follow the accounts, listen to the music, watch the movies/shows, and read the books of the people we love the most. We watch how they live, dissect the drama they are involved in, get ideas from their lifestyle, and even use them as inspiration for who we want to be and what we want to accomplish. There's nothing wrong with having role models, but are we being wise with who we choose to idolize?

I won't spend a lot of time talking about role models because I feel like it's a pretty straightforward point, but we need to keep in mind that influence carries a measure of power with it. When we allow someone or something to influence our decision-making, we're giving that person, object, or obsession a measure of power over us. Don't take for granted how important it is to surround yourself, in person and online, with people who will be a positive influence and set an example of what it looks like to live for Jesus.

3. Manage your time well

Influence is fueled by time. The more time you give someone or something, the greater chance it has of influencing you on a deeper level. Think about the phrase, "We pay attention to them." What is it really saying? The word "pay" in itself constitutes giving, handing over, or transferring. In most cases, when you pay for something, it's for the exchange of something in return. When we say that we pay "attention," we're literally saying that we are giving over our attention in exchange for something else. So the real question becomes, what are we receiving in return for the attention we're paying out? Positive influences or negative influences?

Consider how much time you spend watching or listening to different media outlets, and then decide whether or not that time is being consumed with positive or negative influences. You may have a healthy balance and prioritize your time well, or there might be some changes you need to make in how you invest your time. Remember, every minute counts.

CONSCIOUS VS SUBCONSCIOUS

As we end this section, I want to touch on the topic of conscious versus subconscious and how those two different groups of influences impact our desires.

Conscious influences are the ones we are aware of, the ones we know are happening, and the ones that are obvious, on the surface, and right in front of us. Subconscious influences are the ones that are below the surface and are impacting our thinking without us even knowing it. They can be subtle, indirect, and not obvious until pointed out.

I used to give this example back when I taught my leadership classes. When I walk into a room, my conscious brain picks up what I focus on and bring attention to. Let's say I recognize the lamp turned on in the corner, the slideshow on the tv, and my students looking at me. I'm aware of those things, and I know they are happening.

The subconscious brain, however, picks up everything else I may not have directly focused on but was present nonetheless. Maybe someone was picking their nails, there were three posters on the wall with motivational quotes on them, or there were five rows of desks. Even if I didn't call attention to it, my brain still processed the information.

That's why the subconscious mind is so powerful. It soaks in information we don't even realize it's soaking in. It's why you can go shopping, leave the mall, and have a song stuck in your head. You don't understand how the song got stuck in your head until your friend points out that the song was playing in the last store y'all were in. You may not have realized it at the time, but your brain was internalizing it.

Why do you think companies pay millions of dollars every year in marketing products? You may not think you focused on that "Buy one, get one free" poster you passed when you walked through the aisles at Walmart, but your brain still took notice of it. Commercials, tv shows, movies, ads, branding—it's all intentional. Go look up "subliminal messaging" when you have a chance, and you'll see just how far major companies and corporations will go to make sure their products and agendas are not only getting put in front of you but ingrained in your mind. It's pretty scary, and it's definitely something we don't need to take lightly.

I say all of this to remind you that it's why your parents, pastors, teachers, coaches, and other mentors always tell you to surround yourself with the right influences. Because even when you don't realize it, your brain is picking up and processing and internalizing everything around you—positive as well as negative. The lyrics you hear even when you don't think you are "listening" to the song. The tv show on in the background while you do homework that you're not directly "paying attention to." The accounts you follow and posts you "mindlessly" scroll past. The type of friends you surround yourself with, the news stations you watch, the video games you play, the websites you look at—all of it. Our brains are soaking it in, and whether we admit it or not, it all influences the way we think, talk, and act.

Satan isn't taking this area lightly, so we can't either. If he's intentional about using the influences in our lives to morph our desires, then we have to be intentional about using the influences in our lives to maintain our discipline. Whether it's our relationships, our social standing, or our interest in pop culture, we have to constantly make sure we see the reflection of Jesus. It's the only way to fix our gaze straight ahead and make sure our desires stay focused on Him.

CHAPTER 8 - DISCUSSION GUIDE

Chapter Recap:

We tend to be the most easily influenced by the things we find the most entertaining. This is why we must constantly be aware of how much time, energy, and emotion we are placing in our fascination with pop culture. Three rules of thumb to follow concerning how you allow pop culture to influence you are to create boundaries, choose positive role models, and manage your time well. This will help protect you, consciously as well as subconsciously, from the negative influences of pop culture.

Discussion Questions:

1. Do you set boundaries in your life concerning how you allow pop culture to influence you? Why or why not?

2. What celebrities do you admire the most? Do you think the qualities that draw you to those people are positive or negative, healthy or unhealthy?

3. Consider the areas of social media that have captured your attention the most. Analyze how those areas have influenced your mindset, habits, or lifestyle (whether in a positive or a negative way).

Action Step:

If there is an area of pop culture that has had a negative influence on your life, write down one boundary you can put into place to make sure you maintain the right perspective and balance in that area.

PART 3

The Counter-Attack: Define Your Identity

CHAPTER 9

The Counter-Attack

Once again, Part 1 was all about how to analyze your life to gauge your current threat level concerning how serious you take your relationship with Jesus. Part 2 broke down Satan's strategy for attacking teenagers in today's culture and highlighted three specific areas he will try to influence your desires. Now in Parts 3-5 of the book, we will look at ways you can be intentional about maximizing the threat *you* pose to *him*. It's time for the counter-attack.

When people lie, deceive, or manipulate, it's what they are avoiding that is most important. There's a reason why Satan tells us what he tells us, why he tries to prevent us from discovering certain information, why he paints the narrative the way he does, and why he tries to influence our desires to lead us away from Jesus' best for us.

If Satan is desperate to convince us of something, it's what he isn't desperate to convince us of that should get our attention. It's what he's not telling us that matters. It's what he's trying to steer us away from that carries weight. And that's exactly why we should lock onto those things.

If Satan is trying to hide them, then they pose a threat to hurt him.

So what are those areas? Take a look back at Eve's interaction with the serpent.

From Chapter 5, we saw that Satan wanted to plant a seed of doubt and confusion in Eve's heart, ultimately manipulating her desires so she chose her way over God's way. On a practical level, what was Satan doing? He wanted to steer her away from the truth about who she was (her identity) and God's intention for her (her purpose). And why did Satan succeed in manipulating her desires? Because when temptation presented itself (temptation Eve likely had never encountered to that extent before), she didn't implement the proper strategies to help her overcome it.

When I say the "proper strategies," I mean she wasn't battle-ready with the proactive and reactive strategies that were necessary to withstand the onslaught of the enemy's attack. Eve had God on her side, so she definitely had been *equipped* with the knowledge and tools she needed in order to overcome the temptation, but she hadn't *utilized* those tools in the moment they were most important. Information without implementation is useless.

If we apply those elements to us personally, then it looks something like this: What is Satan trying to steer us away from, make us lose sight of, and prevent us from discovering? Who God says we are (our identity) and who God created us to be (our purpose). And how will we prevent Satan from being successful in manipulating our desires? By developing and utilizing the right strategies needed to defeat him in battle.

Those are the three areas I believe pose the greatest threat to Satan, his demons, and their overall operation: our identity, our purpose, and our strategies.

To engage means to take action, so to form our counter-attack we are going to turn each of these areas into action steps:

~ Define your identity ~ Discover your purpose ~
Develop your strategies ~

We are going to break these three areas down individually in the next three parts of the book to explain what they are, why Satan is threatened by them, and how you can practically apply them to your life. Whether these areas are ones you have a good hold of or ones you badly need to incorporate into your life, I hope you'll pay attention to them and let them sink in. Satan wants you brushing past these things without taking a second glance or slowing down to process them. Don't let that happen. There's too much at stake.

See, Satan has had his moments of being smart. I'll give him that. But he's also dropped the ball in ways he didn't realize at the time. Through stories like the men trying to cast out the demon and the serpent tempting Eve, Satan left breadcrumbs throughout ancient history as to how to defeat him. And we're going to use that insight to our advantage. We now know how Satan operates and how we need to counteract that operation. All that's left is for us to actually get to work. It's time to utilize the power God has equipped us with.

CHAPTER 9 - DISCUSSION GUIDE

Chapter Recap:

When people lie, deceive, or manipulate, it's what they are avoiding that is most important. What is Satan trying to steer us away from, make us lose sight of, and prevent us from discovering? Who God says we are (our identity) and who God created us to be (our purpose). And how will we prevent Satan from being successful in manipulating our desires? By developing and utilizing the right strategies needed to defeat him in battle.

To form our counter-attack, we are going to turn each of these areas into action steps: define your identity, discover your purpose, and develop your strategies.

Discussion Questions:

1. Has there ever been something you feel like the enemy is trying to steer you away from that might pose a threat to him?

2. Think about a time where you were equipped with the knowledge and tools you needed to overcome temptation, but you didn't utilize them in a specific moment to help you achieve victory. What kept you from utilizing them?

3. Even though we haven't explored the topics more in-depth yet, which of the three areas do you already think poses

the greatest threat to the enemy: your identity, your purpose, or your strategies? Why did you choose that specific area?

Action Step:

Take a second to pray and ask God to prepare your heart for what you will read in the following chapters. Specifically, ask Him to reveal to you the area you personally need to focus on the most—identity, purpose, or strategies—in order to be a greater threat to the enemy.

CHAPTER 10

Our Natural Instinct

Let's kick things off with the first step of our counter-attack: define your identity.

I'm in my 14th year of teaching, and years ago I taught a related arts class called Leadership Development. The course was structured to focus on how to develop healthy mindsets, actions, and habits that help you grow as an individual and have a greater influence in society. One of the first topics we discussed was "identity," and I always introduced it by reading an excerpt from a philosophical book called *Sophie's World* by Jostein Gaarder.

The book starts out with a young girl named Sophie coming home from school one day to find a letter in her mailbox. Her name is on the front, but there's no return address or any other information on the envelope. When she opens the letter, she finds a blank sheet of paper with nothing but three handwritten words on it: *"Who are you?"* The book follows Sophie's journey as she investigates this question in pursuit of discovering the answer to her true identity.

This intro always led to a pretty neat discussion. After reading the excerpt, I would ask the students to put themselves in Sophie's place, imagining that they arrived home one day to find a mysterious letter in their mailbox with that single question written on it. Then I would instruct them, "I'm going to go around the room, and when I ask you that question, I want you to answer with the first thing that pops into your brain. Don't process it, don't overanalyze it. Just spit out the first thing that comes to your mind." One by one, I would point at a student and ask them, "Who are you?" and write down their answers on the board.

Most of the students answered with their names (I'm Emily, I'm Gabe, I'm Landree). Many answered with their biology (I'm a boy, I'm a girl, I'm a human being) or with titles related to their family (I'm a brother, I'm a daughter, I'm a cousin). Some answered with categories linked to their education (I'm a middle schooler, I'm a seventh grader, I'm a student), while others answered with hobby-related activities (I'm an athlete, I'm a musician, I'm an artist).

From time to time, I would get answers that were outside the box, but in general very few students ever responded with an answer that went beyond a physical trait, a position, or an activity. You might think it's obvious because, well, what else are they supposed to say? It's not a question you get asked every day. I get that. But if I were to ask each of you that same question, in that same direct manner—*Who are you?*—I bet your gut instinct would be to respond in a similar way.

If you're a Christian and actively pursuing your faith, then you know one of the basic foundations of Christianity is that our identity is found in God and in who He says we are. It was assigned, gifted, and bestowed to us by God Himself. But isn't it interesting that, even though we recognize this, when we ask ourselves the question "Who are you?" we gravitate toward "earthly" responses? Why is that?

It's because it's our natural instinct to define our identity by what we are most known for or what we are most passionate about. Our hard-earned talents, our natural-born gifts, our physical looks, our future dreams, our social media presence, our reputation, our popularity, our personality, our friendships, our family, our job, our wealth, our accomplishments, our failures, our insecurities, or even our past.

Some of these we've chosen, and some of them we're stuck with. Some of them we love, and some of them we'd love to change. Some of these are within our control, and others are beyond our control. Whatever it is we use to define our identity, we're hardwired to think that way because we're human and imperfect. And in a world of distractions and deceits, of consumer cultures and popularity pursuits, it's extremely difficult to consciously acknowledge every day that our identity is found in God alone. That is why it is so important that we not only understand what it means to define our identity in God but also learn how to live from that identity each day.

If you're honest, maybe the answer of "my identity is in God" just isn't good enough, and you tend to focus more on earthly success rather than heavenly significance. Maybe you recognize your identity is in God and you're fine with it, but you have trouble believing it, owning it, and walking in it for whatever reason. Or maybe you haven't quite figured the whole identity thing out yet and you genuinely don't know what your identity is or what it actually means to say "your identity is in God."

No matter what camp you find yourself in right now, I'm praying that these next two chapters bring clarity, confidence, reassurance, hope, joy, and peace.

CHAPTER 10 - DISCUSSION GUIDE

Chapter Recap:

Our natural instinct is to define our identity by what we're most known for or what we're most passionate about. In a world of distractions and deceits, of consumer cultures and popularity pursuits, it's extremely difficult to consciously acknowledge every day that our identity is found in God alone.

With identity comes clarity. You see life clearer, and with this sight comes stability, perspective, and peace. That's why it is so important that we not only understand what it means to define our identity in God but also learn how to live from that identity each day.

Discussion Questions:

1. At this point in your life right now, how do you think others would define your identity based off of what you are known for or what you are most passionate about? Would you agree or disagree with this evaluation?

2. Considering we are created in God's image, why do you think it's our natural instinct to define our identity outside of God?

3. What do you personally find is the most difficult aspect of trying to define your identity?

Action Step:

What would your gut instinct response be if I asked you the question, "Who are you?" Write down your answer and hold on to it. We'll refer back to it at the end of Chapter 12.

CHAPTER 11

So Who Are We?

To define our identity *in* God, I think it's important to first see where we've been tempted to define our identity *outside* of God. This means acknowledging the labels we often slap on ourselves and the "earthly responses" we tend to gravitate toward.

I thought it would be helpful to make a table listing areas we sometimes use to define our identity ("The World's Lies") and then combat them with the truth of what God says about them in the Bible ("God's Truth"). It won't include every area, but it will include some of the major ones. Take some time to read each category to see if there are any that apply to you in particular.

DEFINING OUR IDENTITY	
THE WORLD'S LIES:	GOD'S TRUTH:
I am my family.	You are more than your last name. You are a son and a daughter of the King—a part of my family now. "I will be a Father to you, and you shall be My sons and daughters, Says the Lord Almighty." -2 Corinthians 6:18 (NKJV) "And because we are his children, God has sent the Spirit of his Son into our hearts, prompting us to call out, 'Abba, Father.' Now you are no longer a slave but God's own child. And since you are his child, God has made you his heir." -Galatians 4:6-7 (NLT)
I am my wealth.	You are more than your money and possessions. There is so much more beyond earthly riches. "For the world offers only a craving for physical pleasure, a craving for everything we see, and pride in our achievements and possessions. These are not from the Father, but

	are from this world. And this world is fading away, along with everything that people crave. But anyone who does what pleases God will live forever." -1 John 2:16-17 (NLT) "Don't store up treasures here on earth, where moths eat them and rust destroys them, and where thieves break in and steal. Store your treasures in heaven, where moths and rust cannot destroy, and thieves do not break in and steal. Wherever your treasure is, there the desires of your heart will also be." -Matthew 6:19-21 (NLT)
I am my accomplishments.	**You are more than a list of achievements. I care about the work you are doing for the Kingdom.** "For what good does it do a person if he gains the whole world, but loses or forfeits himself?" -Luke 9:25 (NASB) "I once thought these things were valuable, but now I consider them

	worthless because of what Christ has done. Yes, everything else is worthless when compared with the infinite value of knowing Christ Jesus my Lord. For his sake I have discarded everything else, counting it all as garbage, so that I could gain Christ." -Philippians 3:7-8 (NLT) "But my life is worth nothing to me unless I use it for finishing the work assigned me by the Lord Jesus—the work of telling others the Good News about the wonderful grace of God." -Acts 20:24 (NLT)
I am my mistakes.	**You are more than your failures. I've forgiven you as well as given you a clean slate.** "You were dead because of your sins and because your sinful nature was not yet cut away. Then God made you alive with Christ, for he forgave all our sins. He canceled the record of the charges against us and took it away by nailing it to the cross. In this way, he disarmed the spiritual rulers and authorities. He shamed them publicly by his victory

	over them on the cross." -Colossians 2:13-15 (NLT) "For as high are the heavens are above the earth, so great is His faithful love toward those who fear Him. As far as the east is from the west, so far has He removed our transgressions from us." -Psalm 103:11-12 (HCSB)
I am my fears.	**You are more than what intimidates you. In me, you can find peace, protection, and provision.** "I am leaving you with a gift—peace of mind and heart. And the peace I give is a gift the world cannot give. So don't be troubled or afraid." -John 14:27 (NLT) "Don't be afraid, for I am with you. Don't be discouraged, for I am your God. I will strengthen you and help you. I will hold you up with my victorious right hand." -Isaiah 41:10 (NLT)

	"He will cover you with his feathers. He will shelter you will his wings. His faithful promises are your armor and protection." -Psalm 91:4 (NLT)
I am my past.	**You are more than what's behind you. I'm calling you to embrace all things new.** "Therefore, if anyone is in Christ, he is a new creation; old things have passed away; behold, all things have become new." -2 Corinthians 5:17 (NKJV) "Forget the former things; do not dwell on the past. See, I am doing a new thing! Now it springs up; do you not perceive it? I am making a way in the wilderness and streams in the wasteland." -Isaiah 43:18-19 (NIV) "No, dear brothers and sisters, I have not achieved it, but I focus on this one thing: Forgetting the past and looking forward to what lies ahead, I press on to reach the end of the race and receive the heavenly prize for which God, through Christ

	Jesus, is calling us." -Philippians 4:13-14 (NLT)
I am what I look like.	**You are more than your physical appearance. I pay attention to what's inside of you.** "Don't be concerned about the outward beauty of fancy hairstyles, expensive jewelry, or beautiful clothes. You should clothe yourselves instead with the beauty that comes from within, the unfading beauty of a gentle and quiet spirit, which is so precious to God." -1 Peter 3:3-4 (NLT) "But the Lord said to Samuel, 'Do not look at his appearance or at his physical stature, because I have refused him. For the Lord does not see as man sees; for man looks at the outward appearance, but the Lord looks at the heart.'" -1 Samuel 16:7 (NKJV)
I am worthless.	**You are more valuable than you could ever realize. So valuable that I gave up my Son for you.**

	"What is the price of two sparrows—one copper coin? But not a single sparrow can fall to the ground without your Father knowing. And the very hairs on your head are all numbered. So don't be afraid; you are more valuable to God than a whole flock of sparrows." -Matthew 10:29-31 (NLT) "For you know that God paid a ransom to save you from the empty life you inherited from your ancestors. And it was not paid with mere gold or silver, which lose their value. It was the precious blood of Christ, the sinless, spotless Lamb of God." -1 Peter 1:18-19 (NLT)
I am purposeless.	**You are here for a reason and a purpose. I intentionally created you.** "For we are God's masterpiece. He has created us anew in Christ Jesus, so we can do the good things he planned for us long ago." -Ephesians 2:10 (NLT)

	"You made all the delicate, inner parts of my body and knit me together in my mother's womb. Thank you for making me so wonderfully complex! Your workmanship is marvelous—how well I know it. You watched me as I was being formed in utter seclusion, as I was woven together in the dark of the womb. You saw me before I was born. Every day of my life was recorded in your book. Every moment was laid out before a single day had passed." -Psalm 139:13-16 (NLT)
I am unlovable.	**You are fiercely loved. Nothing can separate my love from you.** "God showed how much he loved us by sending his one and only Son into the world so that we might have eternal life through him. This is real love—not that we loved God, but that he loved us and sent his Son as a sacrifice to take away our sins." -1 John 4:9-11 (NLT) "And I am convinced that nothing can ever separate us from God's

<table>
<tr><td></td><td>love. Neither death nor life, neither angels nor demons, neither our fears for today nor our worries about tomorrow—not even the power of hell can separate us from God's love. No power in the sky above or in the earth below—indeed, nothing in all creation will ever be able to separate us from the love of God that is revealed in Christ Jesus our Lord. -Romans 8:38-39 (NLT)"</td></tr>
</table>

As I considered these categories (and so many other labels we often allow to define us), it hit me that they could all be summarized into three categories: pride, regret, inadequacy. Pride: the tendency to shape our identity around our own strengths, accomplishments, image, or reputation. Regret: the tendency to shape our identity around the mistakes we've made and the failures we've collected. Inadequacy: the tendency to shape our identity around our fears or the self-imposed perception that we aren't good enough.

All three of these things are once again earthly responses that the enemy will try to use to warp our thinking. Like we've said, it's understandable that we gravitate toward those responses because it's a natural instinct. But I hope these tables have made it clear that there is a major difference between the lies the enemy feeds us and the truth that God speaks over us.

By the way, I was thinking about something while writing this chapter that I thought was interesting. When you start a sentence with, "I am," whatever comes next is essentially what you are labeling yourself. (I am my accomplishments, I am an accident, I am worthless, etc.) Here's the thing though: the very words *I AM* is who God called Himself in the Bible. So if you really think about it, you can't begin to describe yourself in a sentence without first describing who God is. As soon as you start to say, "I am," you are already calling on the name of God. Which is a very cool notion to consider because the reality is that your full identity is already contained in Him.

The next time you start to negatively label yourself with the words "I am," stop and imagine you are calling out to God himself. Then instead of filling in the blank with pride, regret, or inadequacy, turn the thought around to bask in the awareness that you are already a reflection of our Savior.

WHAT'S THE BOTTOM LINE?

I think it's important to add context to the topic of identity, but if you're like me then you also want a bottom line, a point-blank response, a straightforward and simple answer as to how to define our identity. If we have accepted Jesus as our Savior and claim to follow Him, then we know our identity is found in Him. But what does that mean exactly? When we say our identity is in God, what are we talking about?

To understand that our identity is in God, we first need to understand that our identity is not about us (which is a little ironic considering it's phrased as "our" identity). God is the one who established our identity, so it was never under our control in the first place. This means we didn't create it, we didn't assign it, and we didn't earn it. Our identity is found in who God is and who God says we are. So what represents God Himself, and what does He have to say about us? I think these verses in Ephesians have our answer:

> |4| Even before he made the world, God loved us and chose us in Christ to be holy and without fault in his eyes. |5| God decided in advance to adopt us into his own family by bringing us to himself through Jesus Christ. This is what he wanted to do, and it gave him great pleasure. -Ephesians 1:4-5 (NLT)

These verses demonstrate that God made some intentional decisions before the world even existed about who we would be. Before we were born, God had already made up His mind about us. God's opinion and perspective were already fixed. This shows that our identity wasn't up for debate. It was predetermined, solidified, and unchanging.

And what were those predetermined decisions? Even before the world was made, these verses highlight that God decided we are *loved*, we are *chosen*, we are *forgiven*, and we are *adopted*.

- We are loved: Before we took a single breath, God chose to love us. That love was so great that Jesus would be sent to die on a cross so we could be found holy and without fault in God's own eyes.

- We are chosen: God didn't need us; He wanted us. He didn't have to choose to allow us to be right with Him, but He did anyway. God made an intentional choice to choose us.

- We are forgiven: We are forgiven through the blood of Jesus Christ. Jesus' sacrifice on the cross erased the gap between us and God, giving us the opportunity and the freedom to dwell with God forever.

- We are adopted: Through God's love and Jesus' sacrifice, God decided in advance to adopt us into His family as His sons and daughters.

To tie it all together, take a look at the last sentence of verse five: *"This is what he wanted to do, and it gave him great pleasure."* God didn't *have* to do these things. He *wanted* to do these things. Getting to love us in this way brought God great pleasure. And what represents pleasure? Happiness, delight, satisfaction, fulfillment, contentment, or my favorite word related to pleasure: *joy*.

When I think about these components—He loves us, He chooses us, He forgives us, and He adopts us—as well as the fact that the choice to do these things brought Him great pleasure, I can't help but think, "Who are we? *We are God's joy.*" That is our identity.

He delights in us. He rejoices over us. He celebrates with us. He sings over us. We bring him happiness. He takes pride in calling us His own. He quickly forgives us again and again because His love and grace never run out. The next time you begin to question who you are, remind yourself that God wanted you. He loves you. He has chosen you. He has forgiven you. He has adopted you. You are His *joy*.

Maybe the following illustration will help solidify this point in your heart...

Similar to a couple verses in the table above, there's another verse where God is speaking to the prophet Jeremiah. God tells him that He knew Jeremiah before He shaped him in his mother's womb (Jeremiah 1:5). I don't know what comes to your mind when you think about God knowing you before you were born, but it conjures up a specific image in my mind.

It makes me think that one day God sat envisioning your life. The texture of your hair, the shape of your nose, the color of your skin, the hue of your eyes. What would make you laugh. What would make you cry. What would make you feel alive and what would burden your heart. The gifts you would be given that would have the potential to change the course of human history. He smiled thinking about your smile. He laughed thinking about your laughter. And in the moment, He fell wildly in love with you.

Then He breathed life into your mother's stomach, and nine months later there you were, crying in your mother's arms. His dream. His miracle. No longer a vision but a reality, moving and blinking in the flesh. His most adored creation. Specifically envisioned, intentionally made.

I don't know where the end of this chapter finds you on the journey to define your identity—certain, struggling, or somewhere in-between—but I want you to know that amidst the insane beauty and awe and wonder of creation, the God of the universe absolutely adores you. That is what it means to be God's joy. And that is exactly who we are.

CHAPTER 11 - DISCUSSION GUIDE

Chapter Recap:

Rather than allowing the world's lies to define our identity by pride, inadequacy, or regret, we need to remind ourselves through God's truth that we are who He says we are. We are loved, we are chosen, we are forgiven, and we are adopted. At our core, *we are God's joy*. That is our identity.

Discussion Questions:

1. Which categories from "The World's Lies" did you relate to the most? Why do you think you struggle with those mindsets in particular?

2. Likewise, which category do you think you've been tempted the most to define your identity outside of Christ: pride, regret, or inadequacy? List specific examples from your life that represent why you chose that category.

3. When you hear that your identity is "God's joy," what images come to your mind, and what emotions do these words invoke?

Action Step:

Like we've discussed in this chapter, we have an identity in Christ that applies to all of us. But considering we are all created uniquely, we also have an individual identity that God will reveal to us if we ask Him. In Jamie Winship's book,

Living Fearless, he tells his readers to simply ask God to give them their specific and unique identity.

Take a minute to pray. First, thank God that your identity is found in Him and that you are His joy. Then, ask God to reveal to you what your specific identity is in Him, and journal what you feel God is speaking to you.

CHAPTER 12

Take It From Gideon

One reason I think we struggle grasping our identity in God is that we don't see things as He sees them. Our perspective isn't His perspective, and it creates a rift between the way we define ourselves versus the way He defines us. I was reading the story of Gideon when the concept of finding our identity in God became clear in an entirely new way for me.

When Gideon is introduced in Judges chapter six, he's privately threshing wheat in a winepress. Why? Essentially, the Israelites had screwed up and God had allowed them to be taken advantage of for years by this group of people called the Midianites. Any time Israel would produce anything of sustenance, the Midianites would take what they wanted and destroy the land, essentially leaving the Israelites impoverished.

So there's Gideon, breaking down some grain in a place normally used to crush grapes, trying to hide it from the bad guys so they won't bully his family and take their food. About that time, the Angel of the Lord visits him and has a few things to say:

|11| Now the Angel of the Lord came and sat under the terebinth tree which was in Ophrah, which belonged to Joash the Abiezrite, while his son Gideon threshed wheat in the winepress, in order to hide it from the Midianites. |12| And the Angel of the Lord appeared to him, and said to him, "The Lord is with you, you mighty man of valor!" |13| Gideon said to Him, "O my lord, if the Lord is with us, why then has all this happened to us? And where are all His miracles which our fathers told us about, saying, 'Did not the Lord bring us up from Egypt?' But now the Lord has forsaken us and delivered us into the hands of the Midianites." |14| Then the Lord turned to him and said, "Go in this might of yours, and you shall save Israel from the hand of the Midianites. Have I not sent you?" -Judges 6:11-14 (NKJV)

Here's Gideon: alone and perhaps intimidated, insecure, frustrated, or questioning a lot of things. At this moment, Gideon is most likely feeling anything but empowered. Yet how does the angel address him? *"You mighty man of valor."* It's almost comical, as if the angel is mocking him. The Bible didn't say it, but I bet even Gideon let out a sarcastic little chuckle when he heard the angel call him that.

Then, Gideon goes on a little mini rant questioning God's motives and miracles. And in the midst of this little pity party, the angel replies a second time, *"Go in this might of yours."* Again, it's almost as if he's making fun of Gideon. Except he isn't. And that's what is so incredible about this exchange.

See, Gideon's predicament had no bearing on God's perspective. The way God viewed him wasn't influenced by the physical, mental, emotional, or even spiritual state that Gideon found himself. Our identity is spiritually assigned, not physically attained, so Gideon's identity was already fixed in God's mind. No janky method of threshing wheat would change that.

From an earthly perspective, Gideon wasn't a mighty man of valor at the moment; but God knew a mighty man of valor is who Gideon was created to be. It's who Gideon was the entire time, even if Gideon's victory hadn't yet caught up with God's vision. Gideon was focusing on the circumstances surrounding him, but God was focusing on the calling within him. And God sees us like that as well. God sees us not as we see ourselves but as who He created us to be in His image all along.

That's the first aspect that struck me with this exchange between Gideon and the angel. But there's a second aspect from the passage that is equally important.

I find it interesting that Gideon gets so hung up on the first thing the angel says (*"The Lord is with you…"*) that he ignores the second thing the angel says (*"…you mighty man of valor!"*). It's like the first part was such a trigger for Gideon, causing his emotions to send him spiraling into his rant, that he ignored the title God had given him. Gideon was so focused on the lack of provision that he overlooked the power of God's proclamation.

I think we can all fall victim to this trap sometimes as well. If we aren't careful, then we can allow our immediate circumstances to stir up our emotions to the extent that we forget, overlook, and even disregard the identity God has assigned to us. Satan is the master of distraction and disorientation, and if we allow emotional confusion or resentment to cloud our judgement then we might miss out on what the Lord is trying to convey to us about who we are in Him.

If we want to be a serious threat to the enemy, we simply cannot allow that to happen.

THE TAKEAWAY

So what can we take away from this passage? Gideon saw himself as a common man, lacking significance, surrounded by an impossible situation. God saw a mighty man of valor, a conduit for the miracles God Himself would perform, a warrior who was going to win unprecedented victories.

In our own lives, we may look at ourselves in a mirror and observe nothing more than raggedy clothes, dirt-streaked skin, and worry-creased lines across our face. But what does God see? He sees mighty men and women of valor, warriors He's created to orchestrate His power and plan through. It's not about people, positions, or preparedness; it's about who God says we are.

I think the story of Gideon is an encouraging reminder that on our worst days where we feel the most invisible, insignificant, and incapable—when we've lost sight of ourselves and aren't sure who we are or what we're supposed to be doing—our identity in Him hasn't changed. We may lose sight of our identity, but God never will. Because in His eyes that's the only way He's ever seen us, and it's the only way He ever *will* see us.

If we're going to adequately understand and fully grasp that our identity is in God, we have to choose to see our identity through His eyes. He's defined our identity, and it's not up for debate. We are loved, we are chosen, we are forgiven, and we are adopted. We are God's joy, and because His perspective is eternal, that truth will never change.

CHAPTER 12 - DISCUSSION GUIDE

Chapter Recap:

The way God views us isn't influenced by the physical, mental, emotional, or even spiritual state we often find ourselves. Our predicament has no bearing on God's perspective. Our identity is spiritually assigned, not physically attained, so our identity is already fixed in God's mind. It's not about people, positions, or preparedness; it's about who God says we are. We may lose sight of our identity, but God never will. Because in His eyes that's the only way He's ever seen us, and it's the only way He ever *will* see us.

Discussion Questions:

1. Why do you think it's easy at times to see ourselves in a negative way or doubt the way God sees us?

2. Have you ever had a "Gideon" moment where you allowed your outside circumstances to influence the way you viewed your identity in God? Explain.

3. How do you mentally, emotionally, or spiritually handle those moments in your life where your view of yourself is different from God's view of yourself?

Action Step:

Now that you have finished Part 3 of the book, reflect on the question again, "Who are you?" Compare the answer that comes to your mind with the answer you wrote down from Chapter 10. Analyze your new answer to see if there has been any more clarity to how you originally defined your identity. Pray that God would help you to maintain the right mindset, attitude, and perspective of your identity as you move forward and grow in your relationship with Him

PART 4

The Counter-Attack:
Discover Your Purpose

CHAPTER 13

Our Approach to Purpose

On to the second step of our counter-attack: discover your purpose.

While your identity is who you are in Jesus, your purpose is found in what you were put on this earth to accomplish. How you fulfill your purpose is determined by what you choose to do with what you've been given. So to discover your purpose, you'll need to first uncover, or become aware of, how God designed you (your "spiritual DNA" you could say). Then, you can take action to greater fulfill your potential in those areas of your life.

Even though the phrase "your purpose" in itself might seem monumental or too big of an idea to grasp, but I promise it's really not so scary if you break it down into smaller steps. And the exciting part is that pursuing your purpose is an intentional act that you can start right now. You don't have to wait until that age, or that phase of life, or that career to discover your purpose. And you definitely *won't* discover it by sitting around cruising through life thinking that one day it will magically appear to you.

Now, let's be real. Some of you can't see past the next Snap or TikTok or Friday night. You can't decide what to eat for breakfast or what to wear to school, more less actually figure out what makes you *you*. You're living for the moment, and the easy answer to "What's your purpose?" is to shrug and say, "How should I know? I'm still young. I've got time to figure all that out when I'm older."

I get all that, trust me. But you're never too young to start figuring some of this stuff out. You can start right now, no matter what age you are or what stage of life you're in. Personal growth is just that—growth. It may change over time, but it doesn't have to stop you from beginning the process. And that's the way your purpose works as well. It may shift or change over time, but you can still start the process of uncovering it right now.

I do want to add something really quick. When I talk about discovering your purpose, this comes with the assumption that you already know you were first created for God Himself. God designed you, created you, and gifted you with the talents, passions, and personality you have today. *He* is the reason you exist, and therefore, *He* is your purpose for existing. These chapters are in no way saying your purpose exists apart from God or that you don't need His wisdom and direction to figure it out. Rather, I'm approaching this chapter with the understanding that we already know our sole purpose is to glorify God with our lives, and we are looking to simply become more aware of the person God created us to be so we can bring Him honor through those areas and be faithful with what He's given us.

With that being said…

One issue I've had with self-help books in the past is that their ideas are very broad and general—great ideas in theory but not very practical. They leave you saying, "Sooo, where do I start?" And I don't want to do that.

I want to be specific with the methods I offer so you can walk away from this book with legitimate answers to the questions and principles discussed.

So I'll introduce a simple approach to how you can go about the process of discovering your purpose, offer a few suggestions on how to apply it in your own life, and share how I applied it to myself to give you a practical example of what the process could look like. Even if you still have questions at the end of it, you'll at least have gotten started.

CHAPTER 13 - DISCUSSION GUIDE

Chapter Recap:

While your identity is who you are in Jesus, your purpose is found in what you were put on this earth to accomplish. How you fulfill your purpose is determined by what you choose to do with what you've been given. You don't have to wait until that age, or that phase of life, or that career to discover your purpose. You can start right now, no matter what age you are or what stage of life you're in. Personal growth is just that—growth. It may change over time, but it doesn't have to stop you from beginning the process.

Discussion Questions:

1. What initial feelings do you get when you hear the question, "What is your purpose?" Do you feel intimidated, overwhelmed, fearful, indifferent, passionate, encouraged, excited, curious? Why do you think that question invokes those feelings in you?

2. Why do you think so many teenagers haven't focused more on starting the process of discovering their purpose?

3. What is one reason you personally have never taken the time to pursue discovering your purpose? If you *have* started the process or believe you have discovered your purpose, what is something thing you have learned so far about yourself?

Action Step:

Even though we haven't gone through the process of how to discover your purpose, if I asked you right now, then what would your answer be to the questions, "What is your purpose? Why do you believe you were put on this earth?" Answer as honest as possible, then hold on to it. We'll refer back to it at the end of the next chapter.

CHAPTER 14

Discovery 101

I don't know how you feel about the entire idea of discovering your purpose—if you think it's daunting, draining, overwhelming, complicated, or even straight up scary—but I want to try and make it as simple and as streamlined as possible. I don't have a magic formula to offer you, but I do have a basic approach that will make pursuing these answers a little less intimidating. We'll start at ground level; then how in-depth you choose to go will ultimately be up to you.

Let's jump right to it. I tried to come up with a fancy acrostic or rhyme scheme to help you remember these components easier, but nothing stuck. So keeping it basic, here it is: If you want to discover your purpose, then combine your *passions*, your *gifts*, your *burdens*, and your *lifelong convictions*.

I'll first talk through each part in a general sense to make sure we are on the same page concerning their definitions. Then I'll move on to how you apply them, present my own personal examples, and finish with a few thoughts on how you can explore things on a deeper level.

FOUR PARTS OF PURPOSE
Your Passions:

Your passions are the activities you love to do. The ones that make you happiest and bring you the most fulfillment and greatest joy. If you weren't in school or at work and could do anything with your free time, these are the things you most likely would be doing. They make you feel alive and add an excitement to your day like nothing else does.

Your passions reflect what resonates with your spirit. The things you are passionate about are the areas you invest the most time, money, effort, and emotion into, and thus have a huge influence on the direction of your life. Your passions are a key component to your purpose because they propel you to pursue your goals, your dreams, and your visions for the future.

Your Gifts:

Your gifts are the talents, abilities, or qualities you feel like you have been naturally gifted with as an individual. These are the areas that other people may have to work hard at, whereas you find them easy to come by. And if you're tempted to think, "Umm, I'm not good at anything," then hold on. Because we're talking about anything that is physically, intellectually, or emotionally driven. Check out these examples:

Maybe excelling in sports or playing instruments comes natural to you; maybe you've always had the ability to communicate well or speak in front of people; maybe you don't have to try hard to do well in a particular subject or academics in general; maybe you're able to be patient, more empathetic, or remain calm in stressful situations; maybe smiling, being positive, or encouraging people has always been easy for you; maybe you find you're able to really listen to people, whereas other people struggle with it.

If we take a step back and analyze our personality close enough, we'll see different areas that flow naturally and organically. Your gifts are an important element to your purpose because they demonstrate the strengths and skill sets you feel God has innately placed inside of you and equipped you with as an individual.

Your Burdens:

When I say what "burdens" your heart, I'm talking about the problems in the world that don't sit well with you, that bother you, or that weigh on you when you see them or hear about them happening. These are the things that don't easily leave your mind, that get you fired up, or that you would immediately fix if you had the time, position, or resources to fix them. Poverty, alcoholism, drug addiction, teen suicide, wars, disease, racism, political corruption, sex trafficking, broken families, and so many more. Your burdens play a significant role in your purpose because they highlight areas that stir your emotions, and anything that stirs your emotions automatically carries the potential for you to take action to do something about it.

Your Lifelong Convictions:

Your lifelong convictions are the mindsets, beliefs, or core values that you can trace back through your childhood, youth, and teenage years. These are the perspectives that haven't dulled with time but have continued to manifest themselves through every phase of your life so far.

Rather than a temporary trend, short-lived fascination, or emotionally-charged view from watching the news, these are the characteristics that have remained consistent throughout your life and have defined you as a person concerning who you are and what your soul resonates with. They may incorporate your beliefs concerning your passions, gifts, and burdens, but they don't have to. They could be other core values that you may not be able to categorize.

For example, maybe from the earliest age or as far back as you can remember, you've sought justice for people who were treated unfairly, enjoyed debating with people or engaging in difficult conversations, had the desire to help people who are in less fortunate situations than your own, been able to make friends easily, earned the trust of people, had the desire to travel the world or start a non-profit organization, been a visionary and created solutions to problems, or sensed that your life serves a higher purpose. (Some of you may have been given a character quality award at school every year when you were younger, and it was always based around the same theme. That might be an example of a lifelong conviction.)

Lifelong convictions help explain why you have a certain perspective on life. One way to say it might be that this is how you are hardwired—causes, ideas, perspectives, or values that you've always felt passionate about or claimed are a backbone of who you are as a person.

Your lifelong convictions are crucial to discovering your purpose because they represent the deepest mental and emotional constructs of your heart and fully encompass who you are as an individual.

APPLICATION

So how do we apply these four parts? It's not necessarily easy, but it's straightforward. The key is to see if you can condense your answers down to arrive at the most simple, basic answer possible.

Whether on paper or electronically, I personally like to keep a journal whenever I do an activity like this. As I get older, I think it's important and beneficial (as well as pretty cool) to look back at what I wrote down at that point in my life. I would encourage you to do the same. Choose a method you like, put the date at the top, and let's take it step by step.

Writing Your Purpose Statement:

Step 1: Write down a short list of your passions, gifts, burdens, and lifelong convictions.

Step 2: Circle, underline, or highlight the most significant or personally meaningful choice in each category.

Step 3: Write a new list with the four items that represent each category.

Step 4: Reword your list to turn it into an action statement: I believe I was created to _______. That is my purpose.

Step 5: Write a list of the things you are currently doing or you could start doing to actively pursue your purpose.

My Personal Example:

I want to give you a practical example of what the process *could* look like, so here is how I implemented the steps in my own life:

Step 1: Write down a short list of your passions, gifts, burdens, and lifelong convictions.

Passions: My passions are reading, writing, traveling/pursuing adventure, instilling value into people (specifically mentoring youth), creating and accomplishing goals, and supporting global ministries.

Gifts: I believe the gifts I've been given are communication skills (teaching, mentoring, writing), the mindsets of determination, discipline, positivity, and encouragement, the ability to connect with youth and help them develop their potential, and the ability to envision the future and then create action steps to accomplish those goals.

Burdens: The things that burden my heart the most are youth feeling a lack of purpose and not recognizing their worth and children globally experiencing circumstances that have stripped away opportunities for them to live a life of abundance and freedom.

Lifelong Convictions: The convictions I feel have been most prevalent throughout my life are the passion for writing, the ability to connect with people and impact youth, *the core belief that we serve a purpose, and the notion that we must live intentionally to make the most of time.*

Step 2: Circle, underline, or highlight the most significant or personally meaningful choice in each category.

Passions: My greatest passion is instilling value into people.

Gifts: I believe my greatest gift could be summarized as connecting with youth and mentoring them on how to develop their potential.

Burdens: The burden that weighs on my heart the most could be summarized as youth feeling a lack of purpose and not recognizing their worth.

Lifelong Convictions: My greatest lifelong conviction would be that we must live intentionally to make the most of time.

Step 3: Write a new list with the four items that represent each category.

The final items on my list representing each category would be instilling value into people, mentoring youth on how to develop their potential, youth feeling a lack of purpose and not recognizing their worth, and the conviction that we must live intentionally to make the most of time.

Step 4: Reword your list to turn it into an action statement:

I believe I was created to instill value into people by helping them recognize their worth, pursue their purpose, and live with intentionality. That is my purpose.

Step 5: Write a list of the things you are currently doing or that you could start doing to actively pursue your purpose.

I am currently a middle school teacher, which in itself provides opportunities every day to instill value into people and mentor youth. I'm also an author, and one aspect of my vision is that a portion of the royalties earned from my books is reinvested into humanitarian organizations to support them financially and help raise awareness for their causes.

Purpose Principles:

Since we are all created differently, the process will not look exactly the same for any single person. Don't get caught up in logistics or legalistic thinking. You don't have to follow each step strictly as they were laid out. The point is that we are starting the process and being intentional about discovering who we are and what we are meant to accomplish.

With that being said, some of you may be asking, "How will I know if I wrote the purpose statement correctly?" That's a fair question, so I wanted to provide a few principles you can use to evaluate your purpose statement to see if it's legitimate.

Here are a few simple ways to check your statement:

1) You will know your purpose statement is legitimate if you read it and agree with it. If you've written a statement that causes you to slow down, reconsider, and question if it's true or not, then there are probably elements to it that you need to look at again. If you read it and immediately say, "Yep, that describes me really well," then you're on to something.

2) You will know your purpose statement is legitimate if it embodies or encompasses all four areas listed above: your passions, your gifts, your burdens, and your lifelong convictions. It doesn't have to directly name each element, but it should reflect all of them in some way.

3) You will know your purpose statement is legitimate if it involves impacting other people. One way to measure if we have been faithful to God is to reflect on what we've done with what He's given us. So naturally, your purpose statement should include at least some element of taking your passions, gifts, burdens, and lifelong convictions and using them to make the world a better place. If your purpose statement just focuses on making your own life better, then you might need to reevaluate where your heart is at in each category and ask God to help you see things through His eyes.

A FEW FINAL THOUGHTS

Sometimes the root of your purpose is broad while how you fulfill your purpose is specific. Using myself as an example, instead of saying my purpose is to teach, mentor, and write, I labeled my purpose as instilling value into people. Instilling value into people is the overarching (or broad) idea, whereas teaching, mentoring, and writing are specific ways I'm using to fulfill that purpose.

With each one of the components in my purpose statement, you could change the location and the occupation, but it still wouldn't change the root of the purpose. Whether I teach middle school, become a youth pastor, or work at a non-profit, I'm still instilling value into people. Whether I mentor students one-on-one, help friends who want to reach their goals, or be the guest speaker at a conference, I'm still helping people pursue their purpose and live intentionally. See what I'm getting at? If your purpose is rooted in a general area, then it doesn't matter what the specific occupation or activity is, it will still fall under the umbrella of what you feel like you have been created to do.

I would encourage you to also not get discouraged or sidetracked if what you are passionate about right now doesn't seem like it fits into a bigger picture. For example, loving basketball might point toward being passionate about athletics or competition in general. Loving shopping might reflect a passion for organization, style, or design. Loving hanging out with friends might represent being passionate about community and connecting with people. You are still figuring a lot of things out, and there's no problem with that.

Remember, you can start where you're at with what you know. You may not know the answers to some of these things. That's fine. What *do* you know? You may not have all of these areas figured out yet. That's fine. What *have* you figured out?

Don't let one small area of confusion or doubt lead you to abandon the entire search. Start with the phase of life you're in with the information you have on hand, and simply go from there.

Your mindset and perspective will most likely change as you grow into your next phase of life, and that's expected. Repeat this process when that time comes and continue to build off the foundation you've already laid. When God sees you taking action and praying through fulfilling your purpose, He will start refining your vision further to where it aligns with His heart. When that happens, you will get even more clarity, courage, and peace of who you believe God created you to be and what you believe God created you to accomplish.

CHAPTER 14 - DISCUSSION GUIDE

Chapter Recap:

If you want to discover your purpose, then combine your passions, your gifts, your burdens, and your lifelong convictions. When God sees you taking action and praying through fulfilling your purpose, He will start refining your vision further to where it aligns with His heart. When that happens, you will get even more clarity, courage, and peace of who you believe God created you to be and what you believe God created you to accomplish.

Discussion Questions:

1. From reading through the chapter, which of the four areas do you think will be the easiest to evaluate yourself, and which one do you think will be the most difficult? Why?

2. Do you think these four areas adequately summarize your purpose, or do you think there are other components that are involved in the process?

3. The third purpose principle is, "You will know your purpose statement is legitimate if it involves impacting other people." How much do you focus on impacting other people? If you focus on it a lot, then why is it important to you? If you don't focus on it as much as you should, why is that?

Action Step:

Complete the exercise in this chapter. Once you are finished, fill in your purpose statement, *"I believe I was created to ______. That is my purpose."* Then compare your purpose statement with the answer you wrote down from Chapter 13. Analyze your responses from both chapters to see how they are aligned and how they are different, then pray that God brings you more clarity, closure, and peace as you pursue living out your purpose every day.

CHAPTER 15

A Lesson from Fordun

As we finish Part 4 of this book, I want to give you one final reason why discovering and pursuing your purpose is so important. We'll do it through a short history lesson…

Have you ever heard of William Wallace? If not, then you've probably at least heard of the movie *Braveheart*, which stars Mel Gibson as Wallace himself. And if you haven't heard of either, then let me summarize it: William Wallace is remembered as one of the greatest heroes in Scottish history for leading an uprising against the English in Scotland's fight for independence in the 13th century. And it's his story that I think gives a beautiful illustration of what it means to fully embody your purpose.

The king of Scotland died in 1286, and by 1290 all other family members who could succeed him to the throne had died as well. King Edward I of England (who had a reputation in history as being ruthless with his enemies) stepped in to "help" oversee who would be selected as the next king of Scotland. However, King Edward had very little interest in allowing the Scots to live free. He started imposing high taxes and demanded that the Scots provide assistance to the English military.

When he was met with resistance, it wasn't long before he moved his forces into Scotland, waged war against the Scots, and officially gained control of the country.[1]

This was the climate that William Wallace was surrounded by—political unrest, limited freedom, a country at war, a country that wasn't his own—and it was in that pivotal time of controversy and unrest that he chose to rise up.

The year was 1297. The town was called Lanark. It was the headquarters of the British Sheriff, who was in charge of administering justice in the surrounding areas. We don't know exactly why Wallace chose to attack here (one myth says that Wallace's wife had been killed by the British and that he wanted revenge), but what we do know is one day Wallace gathered a few men and killed the Sheriff along with his men.[2]

From there, Wallace became the face of the Scottish rebellion. He continued attacking English forts, rallying troops and gaining momentum with each small victory. This wasn't the first act of rebellion the Scottish people had seen, but there was something different about Wallace. He was smart and strategic, utilizing terrain and enforcing guerrilla warfare tactics to outwit his opponents. After a few extensive campaigns, he and other allies were able to regain control of Scottish lands.[3]

The English grew nervous over the territory they were losing, and they sent troops to fight against Wallace. The two armies collided at the Battle of Stirling Bridge in the fall of 1297, where Wallace's army slaughtered the English in a cunning and decisive victory. It was at this point he was knighted the official Guardian of Scotland.[4]

The next year, however, the English would defeat Wallace's forces at the Battle of Falkirk in 1298. With this defeat, Wallace journeyed to France where he is believed to have wanted to secure the French King's assistance in Scotland's war for independence.

Little is known about Wallace for the next few years, but eventually he returned to Scotland and continued his campaign against England.[5]

His career finally came to an end in 1305 when he was betrayed by a fellow Scotsman and turned over to the English. Wallace was tried, convicted of treason, and sentenced to death. King Edward's hatred for Wallace ran so deep that he made sure he experienced a death far more severe than a normal execution. Wallace was first stripped naked and dragged through the streets of London by horse. Then he was hanged, disemboweled, and finally beheaded. His body was cut into several pieces and spread across England as a warning sign to other countries of the consequences of disobeying the King of England.[6]

However, Wallace's death only increased the Scottish drive for revolution. Led by Robert the Bruce, Scotland continued to fight for their independence until they finally gained their freedom from the English in 1328.[7] Even though he wasn't alive to see Scotland's dream come to fruition, William Wallace is still considered one of the most well-known and well-beloved heroes in Scottish history.

Now, why did I tell you all that?

There was a man named John of Fordun who is said to have been the first chronicler to put down what he believed to be the first continuous history of Scotland.[8] And there is something he wrote about Wallace that I think encompasses a crucial aspect of discovering your purpose. Fordun wrote,

"That same year, William Wallace lifted up his head from his den - as it were - and slew the English sheriff of Lanark...From that time therefore, there flocked to him all who were in bitterness of spirit, and weighed down beneath

the burden of bondage under the unbearable domination of English despotism, and he became their leader."[9]

This one line absolutely captivated me the first time I read it: *That same year, William Wallace lifted up his head from his den.*

See, one man held within him the passion, gifts, burdens, and convictions to spark a revolution that would eventually help lead his country to freedom. But for years that purpose went untouched. It lay dormant, still, quiet, undisturbed…until one day he decided to do something about it.

The reason I love this quote by Fordun so much is because it captures the very moment William Wallace decided to tap into the passions, talents, and abilities he had been equipped with, to awaken the hero that lived inside of him all along, to lift up his head and step into the present to seize his purpose. The entire time, his purpose had the potential to change the course of history for generations to come, but it wasn't until he put his purpose into motion and *acted* on it that it was able to come to fruition. Only then was the potential of his purpose fully unlocked.

I couldn't help but think about how all of you reading this book right now have the potential to change the course of human history as well, and what if the only thing stopping you is that you haven't fully discovered (and *acted* on) your purpose yet? You haven't tapped into the passions, gifts, burdens and convictions you've been equipped with? You haven't woken the hero inside of you? You haven't lifted your head to step into the present in order to seize your purpose?

The reality is just like you can't consciously rise out of bed until you stir awake, you can't rise to accomplish great feats without first stirring awake the purpose inside of you. Being aware that you have a purpose is not enough. Recognizing the unique abilities you possess is not enough. Thinking about what you might accomplish through your passions is not enough.

You must call your purpose out from the depths and bring it to life. Awakening requires action, and you can't have action without motion. Thus, fulfilling your purpose requires you to take what you possess and put it into motion to create a better future.

William Wallace would never have accomplished what he did if he hadn't taken action to engage his passions, utilize his gifts, act on his burdens, and embody his convictions. Likewise, our lives will remain stagnant unless we take action to engage, utilize, act upon, and embody our purpose as well.

Why do I mention this story, this quote, this application? Because you need to know the depth of potential that your purpose holds. You have no idea what hangs in the balance of your decision to start this process. There are revolutionaries and visionaries, activists and artists, communicators and creators, world-changers and Kingdom-builders, all waiting to be unleashed.

What are you waiting for?

CHAPTER 15 - DISCUSSION GUIDE

Chapter Recap:

Just like you can't consciously rise out of bed until you stir awake, you can't rise to accomplish great feats without first stirring awake the purpose inside of you. Our lives will remain stagnant unless we choose to engage, utilize, act upon, and embody our purpose. You have no idea what hangs in the balance of your decision to start this process.

Discussion Questions:

1. Are there passions, talents, burdens, or convictions that you have allowed to remain dormant inside of you and that you have never acted on? Why do you think you have allowed those areas to remain quiet for so long?

2. Like Fordun writing of Wallace, if someone were to write a historical article commemorating you one day, what would you want them to say about how you had changed the course of history for your city, your country, or the world?

3. Now that we have finished this section on discovering your purpose, what feelings do you have about the topic compared to the feelings you initially felt when you started reading this section (question #1 from Chapter 13)? If your feelings are the same, why is that? If your feelings have changed, what do you think contributed to them changing?

Action Step:

Choose one area of your purpose that you have not yet acted on, and decide on one thing you will do this week to take action on it. Then take a second to pray to ask God to continue to give you wisdom, direction, clarity, courage, perspective, and peace when it comes to embodying your purpose.

PART 5

The Counter-Attack:
Develop Your Strategies

CHAPTER 16

The Final Piece

Define your identity. Discover your purpose. Now, for the final piece…

Let's say there was a man on the news who publicly announced that 1) his entire purpose of existing was to see you in pain and suffer a slow death, and 2) he wasn't going to rest until he hunted you down and destroyed your entire family (not to mention that there's evidence that he already knows where you live, work, and go to school). What would be your reaction?

You better believe it would grab your attention. You would be on high alert wherever you went. You would take all precautions to make sure you were safe. There would be detectives on your case, a police security detail in front of your home, friends staying with you at all times, your alarm turned on, and perhaps even a weapon by your side. You would pay attention to every location, every environment, every face, every conversation, every detail, and every scenario that could possibly cause you harm.

It's interesting that we would respond to someone in "real life" like that, but we don't respond to Satan in the same way. And we should, because that's exactly how he pursues us. His only purpose for us is to steal, kill, and destroy (John 10:10). I don't think it's out of place to say that Satan and his demons have created an intricate network of operations that branches out like a spiderweb throughout this earth. Information is passed down, and targets are formed. If angels have specific roles, it only makes sense that demons have specific roles as well.

At his core, Satan is the root of our sin. Anything impure or unholy that threatens to create a divide between you and God is in some form or some way Satan's handiwork. The temptations and evil desires are there as a result of the efforts Satan has put in throughout history to see the downfall of mankind. Think about that for a second. His life's work, his legacy, his be-all-end-all, is to see the destruction of the human heart. Therefore, the approach we take to engaging him in battle is vital and cannot be taken lightly.

That's what brings us to the third and final step of our counter-attack: develop your strategies.

When you are preparing to face off against someone in a competition, who poses the greater threat? Someone who doesn't have their act together, isn't prepared, can't defend themselves or their cause, and doesn't know the best method to engage you? Or someone who is sharp, composed, intelligent, detail-oriented, and intentional in their approach and tactical in their maneuvers?

If we want to experience the *abundant* life that is available through Jesus Christ, then we have to develop strategies to fight against the *destructive* life that is waiting with the enemy. And when it comes to developing our strategies, I think they can be broken down into two categories: proactive and reactive.

Creating proactive strategies to prepare for an attack from the enemy as well as creating reactive strategies to defend yourself from the enemy when he does attack. In this last part of the book, we will take a look at proactive and reactive strategies in order to be battle-ready and ultimately maximize our threat level.

WHY SATAN IS THREATENED

Satan hates God. But he can't defeat God, so what's the next best thing for him? He goes after God's most treasured creations: us. It hurts God's heart when we fall away from Him, which Satan loves to see. And as long as we continue to stay blinded from the truth, flail around in the web of his temptations, and slip further into toxic addictions, Satan has us right where he wants us. But the minute we start to figure things out and put up a little resistance? Well, it causes Satan to get all out of sorts.

When we start to develop strategies to fight back against the enemy's plan, it starts to diminish the hold Satan has over us. Those two ideas are directly connected. The more we implement strategies in our daily lives, the less hold Satan has over us. The less we implement strategies in our daily lives, the more hold Satan has over us. It all comes down to the lengths we're willing to go to in order to be prepared for battle.

Have you ever had a strategy going into some sort of competition, and then right out of the gate your opponent does something to throw off that strategy? What happens? You don't know how to respond, you start scrambling to recover, you go on the defensive, and you do whatever it takes to try and survive.

The same is true for Satan. He wants no pushback and no resistance. Why? Plain and simple: he wants easy wins. The more we're prepared to take a stand against Satan, the task of defeating us takes longer, is more strenuous, causes more bloodshed, and slows down Satan's overall campaign. The more time it takes to conquer territory, the less territory he's able to conquer before Jesus comes back and puts an end to his charade. So we must stand in the gap, develop our strategies, and learn how to fight with endurance.

Where do we start with all this? We start with putting on the armor of God.

OUR MAIN STRATEGY: THE AMOR OF GOD

As we begin to face off against the enemy, we have to start with the first, and most important, strategy of all: putting on the armor of God. Putting on God's armor is something that applies to creating both proactive as well as reactive strategies when it comes to counteracting Satan's schemes. It's an umbrella of sorts that all other strategies fall under. So we're going to set the stage for the next two chapters by first introducing what the Bible has to say about it.

|11| Put on the full armor of God, so that you can take your stand against the devil's schemes. |12| For our struggle is not against flesh and blood, but against the rulers, against the authorities, against the powers of this dark world and against the spiritual forces of evil in the heavenly realms. |13| Therefore put on the full armor of God, so that when the day of evil comes, you may be able to stand your ground, and after you have done everything, to stand. |14| Stand firm then, with the belt of truth buckled around your waist, with the

breastplate of righteousness in place, |15| and with your feet fitted with the readiness that comes from the gospel of peace. |16| In addition to all this, take up the shield of faith, with which you can extinguish all the flaming arrows of the evil one. |17| Take the helmet of salvation and the sword of the Spirit, which is the word of God. -Ephesians 6:11-17 (NIV)

A lot of us have heard these verses before, but we need to make sure we know what they mean before we move on. Here's a quick breakdown of each piece of armor:

Belt of truth: Putting on the belt of truth means we are living *from* God's Word and *for* God's Word, which is the source of truth. We are daily walking in God's Word (truth) and intentionally choosing to allow it to define our lives. We are standing firm in its victory and living by its principles. Knowing God's Word illuminates and eliminates the lies of the devil, so when we are secure in God's Word, we are less susceptible to Satan's lies.

A belt in medieval armor surrounded you, held things in place, and carried your weapons. Likewise, God's Word centers you and surrounds you, supports you, and carries your weapon (the Sword of the Spirit).

Breastplate of righteousness: When we put on the breastplate of righteousness, it means we are choosing to live righteously. This includes asking forgiveness for any sins we may have committed as well as asking God to give us strength for the areas we may be tempted to stray from Him. Living righteously means we are making a conscious effort to choose Jesus over the world.

Just like the breastplate of armor would protect your most important organ, your heart, the breastplate of righteousness protects our spiritual heart against the enemy's schemes.

Feet fitted with the readiness that comes from the gospel of peace: Having feet fitted with readiness means we are prepared to take the Word of God (the gospel of peace) and share it with others.

The Gospel was never meant to be kept to ourselves. Jesus' very last command before He ascended into heaven was to spread the Gospel and make more disciples. We must be ready to do this, and that comes from finding a firm foundation in Jesus Christ and the peace He offers.

Soldiers relied on their boots for support when engaging in battle and all other forms of transportation. Our feet must also be ready to support us as we engage in battle against the enemy and aim to complete the tasks God has assigned to us.

Shield of faith: Arming ourselves with the shield of faith means we are having faith that God will provide for us, protect us, and give us the strength we need at the very moment we need it.

A shield was used to protect soldiers from any weapon that might attack them. When we live by faith, God will also protect us against the enemy's flaming arrows.

Helmet of Salvation: Wearing the helmet of salvation means we are reminding ourselves that we have been forgiven, saved, and set free. Our salvation is through Jesus, and He has provided it for us.

Just like the helmet was used to protect a soldier's head, the helmet of salvation is used to protect our mind against Satan's lies and deception. It is a reminder that we belong to God, and God has already won the victory over our lives.

Sword of the Spirit: The sword of the spirit is God's Word itself, the Bible. Utilizing the sword of the spirit means we are using God's word to engage the enemy in battle. To do this, we must be reading it, memorizing it, and applying it in our daily lives.

A soldier's sword was used as his primary weapon against an enemy force. We too must recognize that God's word is our primary weapon against Satan and his demons.

Two ways to apply:

First, we need to "put on" the armor of God by praying to ask God to equip us in these areas. This means we are asking Him to help us walk in His truth, to live righteously, to boldly share the Gospel, to trust and have faith in Him, to stand firm in His salvation, and to engage the enemy through His Word, the Bible.

There's a second piece to this, though. I used to pray to ask God to equip me with new armor every day, which I think we all should do. Then I realized that putting on God's armor can't just be prayers in my heart; it must also be actions in my hands. I first need to pray over these areas to ask for God's protection and provision, but then I need to intentionally pursue growing in each of these areas in my daily life.

This is why putting on the armor of God is both a prayerful act as well as a practical act. In the next two chapters, we are going to explore different proactive and reactive strategies we can use, both of which will be used to put on God's armor every day.

CHAPTER 16 - DISCUSSION GUIDE
Chapter Recap:

If we want to experience the *abundant* life that is available through Jesus Christ, then we have to develop strategies to fight against the *destructive* life that is waiting with the enemy. When it comes to developing our strategies, they can be broken down into two categories: proactive and reactive. Creating proactive strategies to prepare for an attack from the enemy as well as creating reactive strategies to defend yourself from the enemy when he does attack. The first and most important strategy of all is putting on the armor of God.

Discussion Questions:

1. Why do you think we don't often take Satan more seriously?

2. Have you ever really thought about the idea of putting on the armor of God? What part makes the most sense to you, and which part is somewhat confusing?

3. From the descriptions in this chapter, which part of the armor of God do you think is a strength for you, and which part do you think is a weakness for you?

Action Step:

Brainstorm a list of strategies you have developed (if any) for fighting against Satan. Write that list down, and hold on to it. We'll circle back to it at the end of Chapter 18.

CHAPTER 17

Proactive Strategies to Prepare

When it comes to being proactive, we are talking about how we intentionally establish principles to fight against the enemy. Rather than waiting for Satan and his trolls to infiltrate and then choosing how to defend ourselves, we are choosing to prepare beforehand for any attacks that may occur so we can already be in the best position spiritually to hold our ground.

The following strategies are some important tools I've found beneficial for being proactive and practically putting on the armor of God. As you read through this list, check yourself to see if there are things you already do well or if there are things you need to implement in your daily life. We will split it into two categories: *intentional time with God* and *practical daily strategies*.

INTENTIONAL TIME WITH GOD

If a soldier knows he is going into battle the following day, he doesn't wake up to play games, take a bubble bath, and laugh about the latest castle gossip. He wakes up and immediately gets in the right mindset. He makes sure his armor is strong, his weapons are sharp, and his battle tactics are secure. In the same way, we must wake up and immediately get in the right spiritual mindset to start the day (whether your "start of the day" is 8AM or 8PM).

What I've found is that I'm in a much better head and heart space if I start my day with Jesus. You don't know what a day will bring, and being intentional about starting the day with the right mindset will better equip you for the battles you may face. Whatever intentional time with God looks like for you personally, the idea is that we are daily pursuing a better relationship with Him. Here are three categories I think are crucial to incorporate into your lifestyle:

1. Establish an active prayer life

God loves when you spend time with Him, especially when you talk to Him. Long prayers, short prayers, one-word prayers, and everything in-between—God loves it all. And I think all are acceptable, and all have power in their own way and in their own timing.

In the mornings, my prayers typically last a few minutes. When I'm frustrated or stressed at school with a situation, I'll quickly say a one-line prayer. Sometimes when I'm experiencing a special or beautiful moment, I'll find myself praying just two words: "Thank you." And then there have been times where all chaos is breaking loose, and all I have time to pray is, "Help!"

I don't think there's a right way or wrong way to pray, as long as we are genuine and have a pure heart and a pure motive when we pray. Our God is a God who sees, who hears, and who cares. And if we are being intentional about taking time out of our day to talk to our Heavenly Father, our relationship with Him will grow.

Model it after Jesus: Now, some people don't know where to start or what to pray for, and if that's the case then my advice is to model it after the way Jesus said to pray in Matthew 6:5-13. Go to a secluded or quiet place so that you can eliminate distractions and your full attention can be focused on God. Then follow these steps:

1. Thank God for what you've been given.
2. Surrender the day to Him.
3. Ask Him to provide what you need for the day.
4. Ask forgiveness for where you have sinned.
5. Pray for protection against the enemy.

2. Read and memorize scripture

Reading your Bible every day is a beautiful habit to create, both to grow in your relationship with God as well as to gain wisdom into how to live more righteously. I know reading your Bible may seem "basic," but don't overlook just how important it is your spiritual journey. If you don't know where to start, I would choose one of the Gospels (Matthew, Mark, Luke, or John) and begin. Those are the four books that cover the life of Jesus, and considering we are striving to be more like Jesus, I think it's a great place to start reading.

The work doesn't stop there, however. You have to apply it, and one of the best ways to be ready to apply it is to chisel it into the very foundation of your being.

Reading and memorizing scripture is like adding weapons to your arsenal. In a war, soldiers choose the proper weapon depending on the mission or attack at hand. Likewise, we need to be equipped with scripture in order to choose the right verse when we're faced with battles each day. Continuing to live day after day without having any of God's word tattooed on your heart is like showing up to battle without a sword in hand.

When you familiarize yourself with God's truth, it's that much easier to detect the devil's lies. I would analyze where you are the most vulnerable or susceptible to sin and then learn at least two verses that directly target those areas.

A quick note on "time"

Some of y'all are busy. Like, ridiculously busy. And I think busyness can be an easy out for why we don't spend more intentional time pursuing God. The demands of a work schedule, sports practices, homework assignments, maintaining relationships with family and friends, and even going to church can all consume our time in such a way that we feel like we're doing the best we can and there's little time for anything else. The schedule is full, the to-do list is out of control, and the responsibilities are endless. I get it.

But "intentional time" with God doesn't always have to mean sitting down for long stretches of uninterrupted minutes or hours on end. Making intentional time for God is about your heart, not about a checklist. So if you're tempted to say you just don't have enough time, then tap into your resources and see where you *could* make time.

For example, consider…

> *~listening to the Bible on an app while you get ready for school or work*
> *~listening to a sermon or worship music while you exercise*
> *~praying on the bus ride to school or while walking to and from class*

~putting Bible verses in a place where you will see them throughout the day (locker, car, bathroom mirror, etc.)

~centering friend activities around something spiritually related (discussing a book while hanging out, going to a Christian concert, attending a youth event or small group together, etc.)

There's always an excuse not to do something (especially when our time is limited), but if there are excuses to everything, then there are also solutions to everything. You are one of the most creative generations that has ever existed. Get creative!

That being said, there's definitely an element of making sure our priorities are in line. Sometimes I don't think it's if we *have* time or not, it's whether we want to *make* time or not. Like we talked about in Chapter 8, when it comes to managing our time, we have to decide what we're "paying" attention to.

If we're doing our best to handle our responsibilities, be faithful with what God has placed in our lap, and genuinely trying to spend intentional time with Him despite the craziness, He'll bless us for it. I promise. But if we're subtly or subconsciously making the excuse that we just don't have time when in reality our priorities are out of whack, then we've got some rearranging to do.

PRACTICAL DAILY STRATEGIES

Spending intentional time with God is by far the most important piece for being proactive, but there are also practical strategies you can work on to grow your faith every day. These are strategies you can be proactive about implementing that will not only complement your time with God every day but also prepare you for any battles you may face. Each of these areas takes intentionality, and intentionality implies action. If we want to be proactive, we have to act first.

1. Write daily goals and self-accountability

I believe we all need some sort of goal-setting structure in place to help us continually grow daily. For me personally, at the beginning of every year, I choose one word to be the theme of the year. Then I create yearly goals and construct some form of self-accountability to put somewhere where I'll see it every day.

Goals are the tasks I want to accomplish throughout the year. My self-accountability varies year to year based on what I'm looking to accomplish or where I'm looking to grow, but it usually involves some type of questioning or reminders that I use to evaluate myself and hold myself accountable each day.

Here's one example. My focus for this year is the word "Immerse." I won't take the time to elaborate too much, but essentially, I chose that word because I want to fully immerse myself in my identity and purpose when it comes to my faith, family, and writing vision. My goals are in a separate document, but here is what I wrote concerning my questions for self-accountability. I printed this off and placed it by my bathroom mirror to read over while getting ready for school in the morning and getting ready for bed at night.

2026 – Immerse

Morning:

1. What is one thing you will do to practically embody being a Healer of Value today?

2. What is one way you will posture yourself to worship today?

3. What are potential distractions that might tempt you to stray from the mission at hand?

Evening:

1. Whose life did you add value to today?

2. What is one way you loved Megan and Carson Bo today?

3. What is one moment of victory you can build on, and what is one moment of defeat you can learn from concerning how you worshipped today?

Morph this exercise however you want. In my example, the questions are mostly aligned with my focus word of the year. Yours don't have to be. You don't have to have a word at all. Choose one question to ask yourself in the morning and the evening rather than three. Write your favorite poem or Bible verse that inspires you rather than have questions. Create two goals or ten. It doesn't matter. The idea is that you are proactively putting a system into place that helps you grow, improve, reflect, and hold yourself accountable.

Side note: If you've never been intentional about setting goals, there are a lot of different resources to help you do that. One that I think is simple and effective is the "SMART goal" format. Check it out if you're interested.

2. Set up boundaries to maintain healthy influences

In Chapter 8, we talked about the importance of creating boundaries concerning pop culture. Now, we're expanding this category to incorporate all areas of your life. Unfortunately, the reason most people realize they need to set up boundaries is because they've made mistakes that could have been avoided if they had set up boundaries in the first place. Setting up boundaries is a preventative and proactive measure. It's letting yourself, others, and the enemy know where you stand on the front end of a situation. Again, this takes some analyzing and self-reflection in order to know where you might be the most vulnerable for an attack.

Setting boundaries usually isn't easy, fun, convenient, or even comfortable, but it's necessary and wise. If you're struggling with specific boundaries to put into place, just remember that your most strenuous "no's" are your most significant precautions. The harder it is to say no to something probably means that that specific thing is really tempting or has a great amount of potential to control your life. The more difficult it is to navigate through putting a boundary in place, the more likely it is that the boundary is that much more important to your spiritual life.

So what areas do you need to set up boundaries? Here are a few off the top of my head that might apply to you. Maybe you need to set up boundaries with…

> *~how far you go physically with the person you're dating*
> *~what websites or social media accounts you look at*
> *~the environment you place yourself in (house parties, sleepovers, etc.)*
> *~the amount of alcohol you drink*

~the movies/shows you watch and the music you listen to

~how you choose to present yourself (in person and online)

~the time you invest in friendships that may not be good for you

~the video games you play

~the amount of time you spend across social media platforms

~where and how you communicate with people in general

Temptations are often the most powerful when they are right in front of us, and that's why we have to be extremely aware of the situations we are placing ourselves in and the influences we allow into our lives. It's one of the most important reasons for setting up boundaries. Creating boundaries naturally monitors the environments you place yourself in and the influences you allow to impact your thinking.

If you want to get really basic with it, setting up a boundary is simply saying, "No, I won't do that. That's as far as I'll go." You're smart enough to know what situations, areas, or groups of people tempt you the most and how to put measures into place to hold yourself accountable. The real issue usually isn't whether or not we are aware of boundaries we need; it's whether or not we actually have the discipline to do something about them. Choose wisely.

3. Get connected with a healthy community

When I think back to my high school years, one thing I'm extremely grateful for is that I had a solid church and youth group that I attended regularly (two areas I didn't consistently make a priority in college, and my spiritual life suffered for it). Piggybacking on what we talked about concerning relationships in Chapter 6, one of the most important things you can do is surround yourself with the right people. In this case, I'm talking about getting connected with a healthy community through finding a church to attend and getting plugged into a youth group there. These two areas in particular will help you grow closer to Jesus and hold you accountable throughout the week.

We need multiple sources of God's Word pouring into us. We need to have our own intentional time with God, but we also need to be mentored by people who are older, wiser, and can offer different perspectives about how God says to live. When you're consistently going to church and participating in a youth group, then you're placing yourself in an environment to learn, grow, worship, serve, and overall pursue your faith with a like-minded community. It takes effort and intentionality, but we must make it a priority.

This point also circles back to what we talked about in Chapter 6 and the importance of surrounding yourself with the right people. When you're consistently in the right environment and surrounding yourself with friends, worship leaders, and pastors who want God's best for you, it automatically decreases the opportunities Satan has of leading you off course. If you place yourself in a half-lit room, there will be a lot of shadows. But if you place yourself in a room full of light, the shadows have nowhere to hide. We need to constantly strive to develop relationships with people who will pour light into us, and you simply won't get those if you aren't intentional about the health of the community you build.

On that note, this isn't about simply checking a box. It's not enough to go to church and join a youth group just to say you do it. There are a lot of "church" people who don't do church things. (One of my best friends once told me that the first time he smoked weed was at church camp.) This is about recognizing that you need to be connected to a healthy community and then actually pursuing growth in your daily walk with Jesus once you are there.

We all need help in this life, and we live better when we're connected.

CHAPTER 17 - DISCUSSION GUIDE

Chapter Recap:

When it comes to being proactive, we are talking about how we intentionally establish principles to fight against the enemy. Rather than waiting for Satan and his trolls to infiltrate and then choosing how to defend ourselves, we are choosing to prepare beforehand for any attacks that may occur so we can already be in the best position spiritually to hold our ground.

Key proactive strategies are to daily spend intentional time with God (praying, reading the Bible, memorizing scripture) and implementing practical strategies (creating goals and establishing self-accountability, setting up boundaries, and getting connected with a healthy community).

Discussion Questions:

1. Why do you think it's important to be proactive in your approach to spiritual warfare?

2. What do you think is the most challenging aspect of proactively preparing strategies to engage the enemy?

3. Out of the strategies listed in the chapter (praying, reading and memorizing scripture, writing goals and self-accountability, setting up boundaries, and getting connected with a healthy community), which one would you consider a

strength and which one would you consider a weakness for you personally?

Action Step:

Consider the difference between not "having" time and not "making" time. Choose one area you know you could reinvest your time wiser in order to make more intentional time for God every day, and make that change this week.

CHAPTER 18

Reactive Strategies to Defend

The truth of the matter is no matter how well you have prepared and equipped yourself with the proactive strategies you need to engage the enemy, nothing compares to when you actually encounter Satan and his demons on the battlefield. It wouldn't be a battle unless both sides were clashing against each other, so the very essence of going into battle means you will be forced to defend yourself at some point. Now that you've developed proactive strategies, it's time to talk about reactive strategies.

When we say "reactive strategies to defend," we are talking about protecting yourself in the moment of an attack, taking a personal hit without letting it crush your armor, or absorbing a blow and recovering before a gap is created in the front lines of your spiritual guard.

I've listed a few basic strategies below that are very important when coming face-to-face with the enemy in real time. Keep in mind, any strategy will remain only a strategy as long as it is sidelined. Each of the following strategies is meant to be put into action and made practical in your daily life. As you read through this list, already begin brainstorming what each one might look like for you personally.

1. Pray First

I think it's interesting that when we experience frustration or temptation our gut instinct is to immediately react out of emotion rather than to respond with prayer. It's human nature to respond instinctively, I get it. But here's one thing I've learned about us as human beings: when it comes to any type of pain or conflict, what we turn *to* shows what we place our faith *in*. Or in some cases, *who* we turn to shows *who* we place our faith in.

What is your first instinct when someone makes you mad, when an expectation isn't met, or when you experience pain? Who or what do you turn to in those moments?

We have to develop the mental and spiritual discipline to turn to God *first* whenever we encounter some type of attack from the enemy. There's no other way around it. This doesn't mean you pray and then ignore other people's advice or push aside friends who are trying to help you. It means you go to God first for help, *then* you move forward.

This only comes with practice, so try to catch yourself the next time you see the enemy trying to defeat you and choose to pray your way through it first. I guarantee you'll start seeing things with a different perspective, win more battles, and live with less regret.

2. Utilize scripture in the moment of attack

If you've been intentional about memorizing scripture verses for different areas of weakness or temptation, then when the attack comes you should already be prepared to defend yourself against the enemy. Choose the verse that most correlates to what you are encountering, and claim it in the name of Jesus. Quoting scripture helps you speak God's truth, claim God's victory, and walk in God's freedom.

Again, it would be pointless to memorize those verses if you didn't actually utilize them, so one key is to get into the habit of making prayer and quoting scripture the first thing you turn to in a moment of frustration, temptation, or distraction.

3. Shut down the thought before it spirals out of control

I want to spend a little time on this one.

Have you ever remembered something that made you angry and started dwelling on it—what you should have said or should have done and what you would do or say if it happened again—and then before you know it you're furious again and punching a pillow? Or maybe you have one discouraging thought that opens up your mind, and soon you find yourself in a dark place and bad head space. Or maybe it's a lustful thought, and suddenly you're obsessing over something you have no business obsessing over and going down a dangerous road you never thought you'd travel. This is what we're talking about when we say a "thought spiral" or thought spiraling out of control.

We have to develop the discipline to shut down intrusive thoughts before they spiral out of control and lead us to sin. Whatever the thought may be—fear, anger, pride, jealousy, bitterness, insecurity, lust, regret, or discontentment—it's crucial that we deny it before we dwell on it, or else we could allow it to lead to further action that could be hurtful to ourselves and others.

In 2 Corinthians 10:5, it says, *"We destroy arguments and every lofty opinion raised against the knowledge of God, and take every thought captive to obey Christ"* (ESV). To take every thought captive and shut it down means that when a negative thought enters your mind, you immediately stop yourself from dwelling on it, surrender the thought to God, speak His truth and victory over it, and redirect your thinking to something powerful, uplifting, and renewing.

Eve's example:

What does it look like to let a thought spiral out of control rather than shutting it down? Think back to the story I referenced in Chapter 5 when Eve fell to temptation. Remember how Eve handled it? It wasn't as simple as "she gave in," or "then she sinned." It doesn't jump straight to "she took the fruit and ate." There's more to it than that.

Take a look at verse six: *"Then the woman saw that the tree was good for food and delightful to look at, and that it was desirable for obtaining wisdom. So she took some of its fruit and ate it; she also gave some to her husband, who was with her, and he ate it"* (Gen. 3:6, HCSB).

Go with me here. When the serpent starts talking about how Eve's eyes will be opened and she'll know good and evil, you can almost see Eve slowly turning her head and facing the tree, the serpent's voice soothing and calm, maybe even trance-like. She listens as he presents information she's never considered before. Perhaps for the first time, she *really* looks at the tree. And where do her thoughts go?

"I mean, the tree does have great fruit, and you need fruit for food. It's also a beautiful tree. Surely, it's not that threatening. And could it really give me wisdom that I've never had before? These are all good things, right?" Who knows if that was what her inner dialogue looked like, but the point is that her thought process is what led her to eventually give in.

How did all this happen? How do you go from being content with your Creator and living a life of perfection without worry or fear, to choosing to turn your back on your Creator and throwing away everything He provided for you? It's pretty straightforward, really: Eve was willing to entertain the thought, which opened her up to sin.

Maybe it's happened to you before. You've been tempted to make a decision you knew was wrong, and at first you resisted the temptation. But then you second-guessed it and began to rationalize it in your mind until it made sense. Or maybe you started to stack the evidence of why it was okay, why it ultimately wouldn't be that bad, or why no harm would come to you if you made the decision. Any time you linger too long on a thought rather than shutting it down, you will inevitably begin dwelling on it and rationalizing why it isn't so bad.

I think Eve did this. When the devil tempted her, she didn't rebuke him, tell him to run along, get righteously angry and demand he leave her alone, or even call out to God to come intervene.

She was willing to entertain the thought, which opened herself up to it, leading her to linger on it and begin rationalizing why it wasn't so bad. That's what a thought spiral does. It starts with one thought, which leads to another thought, and another and another until it's spiraling out of control.

A personal example:

What does it look like to shut a thought down? Let's use a real-life example to apply it.

I lived in Indonesia for two years. Whenever we had the chance, we would fly one island over to the island of Bali for a weekend getaway. While it was always fun going to the beach, you also had to mentally prepare yourself for one specific element: from the time you arrived at the beach until the time you left, there would be a constant flow of native islanders trying to sell you things. Jewelry, hand-woven wristbands, T-shirts, massages, ice cream bars, drinks, souvenir trinkets, and more. You name it, they had it. And if they didn't have it, then they would go find it for you.

What made this interaction so tedious is that it took a lot of work to get them to accept "no" for an answer. You had to refuse multiple times before they would allow you to continue walking, and even then, they often circled back to you once you found your spot on the beach and settled in. It was pretty annoying, actually, considering all we wanted to do was relax and enjoy some time to ourselves.

It wasn't until we had traveled to the beaches a few times that we learned how to solve this issue. If you wanted to get your message across and not be bothered, then you had to shut them down before they even had the chance to get going. Like, hard shut down.

As in, hand up to stop them from approaching you, firmly tell them you didn't want anything, refuse to look at them again, ignore any of their attempts to try and get your attention, and keep moving in the direction you were going.

If you paused to talk, hesitated to consider, lingered at all, or showed any inkling of a sign that you might be interested in what they had to offer, then you would never get them to leave you alone. (Especially, if you bought something. If you bought something from one person, then the rest thought you would buy something from them as well.) You couldn't even smile, or be polite, or kindly decline them. It had to be a hard shut down where they immediately knew there was no chance that you would do business with them. So we had to learn to give a direct answer, look straight ahead, and keep moving forward.

I'm fully convinced that one of the greatest tactics of the enemy isn't to immediately drown you in sin. He's smarter than that. He knows you won't fall for it. You're too grounded. So how does he approach it? Just like in the case of Eve, he tries to get you to pause for even the slightest moment to take a second glance. He tries to get you to hesitate and reconsider. He tries to get you to at least be open to entertaining the thought or the decision. If he can do those things, then he's got his foot in the door. That's what he wants. If he can get a foot in the door, he can wedge his leg inside. With a leg inside, he can push his way in until he gets enough strength to force his entire body into the house of your heart.

So what do we need to do? Completely shut him down. A hand up-firmly saying no-refusing to look in his direction-ignoring his attempts to get your attention-keep moving forward kind of shutdown. Solomon once wrote, *"Let your eyes look straight ahead; fix your gaze directly before you. Give careful thought to the paths for your feet and be steadfast in all your ways. Do not turn to the right or the left; keep your foot from evil"* (Prov. 4:25-27, NIV).

As the popular saying goes, "Don't let the distractions distract you." Refuse to entertain the thought. Refuse to open yourself up to the sin. Don't let one thought spiral to destruction and take you with it. Move your shield into place, block the blow, and keep moving forward.

4. Have an activity that helps redirect your thinking

If you shut down a thought and don't let it spiral but you don't have another thought to replace it, then you will quickly return to the temptation and begin dwelling on negative thoughts again. Something has to fill your thoughts, so you have to make sure that *something* is going to help you instead of hurt you.

That's why I think it's critical to physically have an activity that redirects our thinking and helps us gain perspective again. It's difficult to mentally redirect your thinking if you don't physically change your environment. This means you need an activity, an interest, a hobby, a dream, a vision, *something* you can physically engage in that will help get your mind off the current situation, circumstance, or temptation.

Our minds operate differently when we engage in different activities. If you want to think about something else, then *do* something else. It's basic science. But if you genuinely have found what you believe to be a higher purpose or calling—something that you're passionate about and that motivates you—then that's especially important because it gives you a new perspective of what you allow to absorb your time, energy, and emotion.

There's a familiar story in the book of Nehemiah where he returns to his home city of Jerusalem to help rebuild the city's wall.

Rebuilding the wall was Nehemiah's focus, his goal, his higher calling, his significant pursuit. Once the construction was underway, there were men who attempted to distract him, intimidate him, threaten him, and ultimately prevent him from accomplishing his task. At one point, they asked Nehemiah to leave his work and come down off the wall to talk to them (with the intent to kill him). What was Nehemiah's response? *"And I sent messengers to them, saying, 'I am doing a great work and I cannot come down. Why should the work stop while I leave it and come down to you?'"* (Nehemiah 6:3, ESV).

In other words, Nehemiah recognized the distraction and their intent to harm, and instead of getting involved with their mess, he decided to stay focused on the mission at hand. He recognized he was trying to accomplish something of value, something of greater significance, and he didn't have *time* to stop the work. There were more important things at stake.

Or as it says in 2 Timothy 2:3-4, *"Endure suffering along with me, as a good soldier of Christ Jesus. Soldiers don't get tied up in the affairs of civilian life, for then they cannot please the officer who enlisted them"* (NLT). These verses remind us to stay focused on the mission at hand and to not allow ourselves to be distracted by things that would devalue our worth or our position in God's army.

If you've been called to accomplish God's tasks, then anything else you get "tied up in" will be settling for less than your value in Christ.

I think this is an important aspect of engaging in an activity that redirects our thinking. If we are so focused on what we believe we were created to do, then we literally don't have time to fool around with temptations or be mentally preoccupied with any other distraction from the enemy. There are simply more important things at stake.

Redirecting your thinking is much easier when you have a particular activity you can turn to that brings you joy and a sense of purpose (another reason why discovering your purpose, from Chapter 14, is so important). So find something you're passionate about and develop the discipline to pursue those activities when your spiritual battles heat up. You'll find that you will not only have more victories, but you will also accomplish things of much greater significance for the Kingdom than you ever would have accomplished by wasting your time on fruitless thoughts and activities from the enemy.

5. Contact something you trust (your "threat level partner")

I think we all need at least one person we can be completely transparent and vulnerable with concerning the areas in which we are struggling and the battles we are fighting. Someone who will listen, encourage, support, hold us accountable, and pour wisdom into our lives. Someone we can confide in without fear of judgement or betrayal. Someone who will go to battle with us and not shy away from the intensity of the fight. We're going to call that person your TLP—your "threat level partner").

Do you have a friendship like that in your life? And I don't mean a "ride or die" who will follow you and support you blindly. (After all, if the person you're constantly getting into trouble with is the person you consider your TLP, then you don't really have a TLP. You just have a PIC—a "partner in crime.") I'm talking about a person who cares about your threat level and doesn't want to see it diminished. I'm talking about a person who will do anything to help you get to the feet of Jesus (think back to what we said about choosing your friends wisely in Chapter 6).

After you've established that relationship of trust and accountability, then the next step is to actually have the courage to contact that person at the very moment you're battling against the enemy. Text them and ask them to pray for you. Call them to chat to simply help you redirect your thinking. Meet them so you can hang out, share your heart, and get advice. As Proverbs says, *"As iron sharpens iron, so one person sharpens another"* (27:17, NIV).

We weren't built to fight these battles alone. The sooner we allow someone into our inner circle, the quicker the enemy will see we mean business. There's nothing like positive peer pressure to encourage us to stay on the right track. Find your TLP, and go to battle together.

TOTAL VICTORY

To end this chapter, I want to apply what we've talked about with one last Bible story.

I was reading in the book of Joshua where the kings of the Amorites joined forces to try and attack the city of Gibeon. The Gibeonites sent word to Joshua to ask for military support and that he rescue them from being wiped out. Joshua responded to their request and brought his entire army to face the armies of the Amorite kings.

The Lord gave Joshua victory that day, forcing the five Amorite kings to flee to caves in a nearby hill country. Joshua had the stone rolled away from the cave and the five kings brought in front of him. Then this happened:

> |24| When they had brought these kings to Joshua, he summoned all the men of Israel and said to the army commanders who had come with him, "Come here and put your feet on the necks of these kings." So they came forward and placed their feet on their necks. |25| Joshua said to them, "Do not be afraid; do not be

discouraged. Be strong and courageous. This is what the Lord will do to all the enemies you are going to fight." [26] Then Joshua put the kings to death and exposed their bodies on five poles, and they were left hanging on the poles until evening (Josh. 10:24-26, NIV).

This was the catalyst that launched a massive military campaign for Joshua and the Israelite army. Following this encounter, Joshua's army swept through and conquered each city in the region and surrounding area. And with each city they defeated, the Bible records the same strategy: Joshua killed them by the sword, completely destroyed them, and left no survivors.

This story gave me such good insight to the type of warfare mentality I need to adopt. When it comes to fighting against Satan and his demons, there can be *no* reluctance, *no* hesitation, *no* compromising, *no* second-guessing, *no* reconsidering, *no* lingering, *no* opening up, *no* entertaining, *no* mercy, and *no* partial victory. We must step on the enemies' necks, destroy them with God's sword, wipe them out completely, and leave no survivors. There is no letting them hang around or take one more breath of fresh air. Total victory is the only option. *That's* how you mount a defense and wage war against the enemy when he attacks.

Praying first, utilizing scripture, shutting down thought spirals, redirecting our thinking by pursuing a higher vision, and contacting someone you trust for accountability are all ways to reactively mount a defense when the enemy attacks. Concerning the armor of God, all of these methods help you stay grounded in the truth, pursue righteous living, remain steadfast in your faith to block the enemy's attack, steady your feet so you can continue moving forward, secure your confidence in the salvation of Jesus Christ, and re-engage the enemy by counter-attacking.

Whether it's acting proactively or reactively, it's up to us to make sure we're equipped and prepared to engage in spiritual warfare. Some things you can't get bypass, can't sneak past, and can't find an easier route around. Some things you have to face head-on, and so it is when it comes to standing your ground and becoming a serious threat to the enemy.

Do you think you're ready?

CHAPTER 18 - DISCUSSION GUIDE

Chapter Recap:

When we say, "reactive strategies to defend," we are talking about protecting yourself in the moment of an attack, taking a personal hit without letting it crush your armor, or absorbing a blow and recovering before a gap is created in the front lines of your spiritual guard.

Key reactive strategies are praying first, utilizing scripture, shutting down thought spirals, pursuing activities that redirect your thinking, and contacting someone you trust for accountability.

Discussion Questions:

1. What do you think is the most challenging aspect of defending your heart against the enemy's attacks?

2. Out of the strategies listed above (praying, utilizing scripture, shutting down the thought, engaging in an activity to redirect your thinking, or contacting someone you trust for accountability), which one would you consider a strength and which one would you consider a weakness for you personally?

3. Now that we have finished this section, do you think it's more difficult to proactively prepare for the enemy's attacks or reactively respond to the enemy's attacks? Why is this area the most difficult for you personally?

Action Step:

Look back at the list of strategies you wrote down from Chapter 16 and compare it with the strategies listed in these last two chapters. Are there items you need to add or replace on your list? Take a few minutes to create a final list of strategies that resonate with you and that you believe will help you become a greater threat to the enemy.

CONCLUSION

A Call to Action

We've talked about how to evaluate your threat level and why it matters to Jesus' overall mission. We've done a little demon reconnaissance work to take a deeper look at who Satan is and what his main strategies are for attacking you. We discussed different areas the enemy will typically try to influence you the most at this stage of your life. Then we formed a counter-attack and evaluated the three areas where you can be the biggest threat to the enemy.

So, what now? How do we end all this?

WHAT'S IN A NAME?

There's a story about Alexander the Great that has been passed down through the years that I think perfectly encompasses the emotion of what we've been talking about.

Alexander the Great was the king of Macedonia from 336-323 B.C. and is considered one of the greatest military and diplomatic minds in ancient history. At the time of his death, he had conquered most of the known world at the time, his empire stretching three continents and covering over two million square miles.[1]

Alexander the Great was relentless in his pursuit of victory and success. By utilizing different combinations of military units, implementing innovated military strategies, and tactically using the terrain around him, he created one of the largest empires in history.[2] To fight in his army meant that defeat was not an option. If there ever was a picture of loyalty, bravery, and endurance, it was Alexander the Great.

But there's a story not many people have heard about him. A story that, like all good stories, might be dipped in a bit of legend and myth passed down through the generations—we're not sure—but it's powerful, nonetheless. It goes a little something like this…

One day, Alexander was in his tent when two of his commanders walked in dragging a soldier between them. They walked up to Alexander's throne and threw the soldier at the feet of their king. Alexander looked on in bewilderment. "What's the purpose of this?" he asked.

One of his commanders responded, "Sir, this man refuses to fight. He simply won't engage the enemy. We even caught him trying to escape."

Alexander eyed the man and scoffed. "A soldier in my army who won't fight? Surely, you must be joking?"

The commander shook his head. "I'm afraid not, sir."

Alexander looked down at the pitiful looking soldier. "What's your name, son?"

"My name is Alexander, sir," the soldier said quietly.

At the mention of his name, Alexander the Great stood up and started laughing. "What did you say your name was?"

The soldier remained in place, cowering on the ground. "M–My name is…Alexander, s-sir," he stammered in fear.

Alexander the Great's face recoiled in disgust. "No, no, no. That *can't* be your name. See, *my* name is Alexander. Alexander the *Great!* So your name can't be Alexander as well. I'm going to ask you one more time, soldier, what is your *name*?!"

At this, the soldier let out a pitiful whimper. With small tears coursing down his cheeks, his shoulders sank in utter defeat. He whispered, "My name is Alexander, sir."

You see, Alexander the Great couldn't grasp that someone with his same name would stand for everything that he as a king stood *against*, that a soldier in his own army would represent the opposite of everything that he represented himself. It was simply inconceivable to him.

The story goes that Alexander the Great finally stood up, pointed a finger down at the young soldier, and with a calm determination said, "Boy, either you change your conduct, or you change your name."[3]

Either you change your *conduct*, or you change your *name*.

It saddens me to think about how many times I've hurt the cause of Christ because I claimed His name with my words but then showed no sign of Him by the way I lived. To think of the times I called myself a Christian but then turned around and lived a lifestyle opposite of what Christ looks like. And the reality is that that kind of hypocrisy is simply unacceptable in light of what the gospel represents.

It sounds extreme, but it's not too far off to say that either we start acting like a Christian or we quit calling ourselves one.

But what about grace? What about forgiveness? We all make mistakes, right?

Yes, we're not perfect. We all fail. And when we do, Jesus is standing there with His arms open, ready to welcome us home and pour out His love on us. But when we get to the point where being a "Christian" is merely a title rather than a testimony, we are no longer talking about simple grace or forgiveness; we're talking about a safety net that we think enables us to live as we choose while still having Jesus waiting on us at the end of the day. That was never how Jesus intended it to be. Our relationship must be rooted deeper than that. And until it is, our threat level will remain nonexistent.

So it's decision-making time for all of us. What's it going to be? A conduct change or a name change?

RECLAIM YOUR TERRITORY

When I was in high school, our youth building sat next to a children's playground. Usually, the younger kids had already been released and were outside running around by the time the high schoolers let out.

One Wednesday night, I stepped outside after our service ended to see kids running around the playground, laughing and yelling. I don't know what the game was called that they were playing (if they were even playing a game), but there was one kid running around with his hands cocked like a gun "shooting" at the other kids. If he "shot" you then you were supposed to fall down and die. Of course, all of the kids were going along with it because that's what kids do—they obey the unspoken rules of the game.

Except for one kid.

His name was Josiah, and he was no older than five or six years old. When I walked outside, I remember seeing him standing nearby watching the other kids run around playing. I'm not sure if he was confused or curious, but he wasn't participating.

Suddenly, the kid with the finger-gun ran up to Josiah, pointed his hands at him, and let the bullets fly. *Pew-pew.* Josiah didn't move. The kid stood his ground and fired again. *Pew-pew-pew.* Again, Josiah just stared back, not moving. The kid seemed a bit annoyed and yelled at Josiah, "Hey, I shot you! You have to fall down!" Again, Josiah didn't say a word. He just stood there, staring. It was almost as if he didn't understand the concept or rules of the game.

I was watching the entire thing unfold, and I started laughing. I looked at Josiah and said, "Tell him, Josiah. Say I'm not dead!" Josiah looked at me, then looked at the kid, and this understanding seemed to pass over his face. He turned to the kid and calmly said, "I'm not dead."

The kid tried to shoot Josiah again, but again Josiah repeated, "I'm not dead." Then Josiah began repeating the phrase over and over, each time growing louder and more confident. "I'm not dead…I'm not dead…*I'm not dead!*" Surprising enough, the kid who had been so bold before turned and began running away. But Josiah wouldn't let it go. He started chasing the kid around the playground yelling after him, "I'm not dead! HEY! I'M NOT DEAD!"

And while laughing at this silly exchange taking place, I was suddenly struck with a powerful realization. In the game of life, when temptations and trials come our way, when Satan shoots his fiery darts at us, what do we often do? We get swept up in the moment and don't throw up our shields. We take the hit and fall down. We bend to his wishes, we surrender to his schemes, and we wilt under the pressure of spiritual warfare. And after we've conditioned ourselves to obey his rules time and time again, it gets easier and easier to take the shot and remove ourselves from contention of being any threat to the enemy.

But I wonder what would happen if we no longer played by Satan's rules.

What if we were no longer so easily satisfied by the things of the world and no longer settled for anything other than God's best for us? What if—as we're lying on the ground after falling to yet another temptation, watching Satan turn his back and moving on to someone else—we called out to him, "Hey Satan! Hold on." And as he stopped in his tracks and slowly turned around, we stood back to our feet, dusted ourselves off, and said to him, *"I'm not dead."*

I can see Satan, confused, bewildered, perhaps even jeering at us because he's not taking us seriously yet. But what if we said to him, "See, you thought I was beyond saving. You thought I was lost for good. You thought you had destroyed me.

You thought you had enslaved me in that mindset, that habit, that addiction. You thought you had *won*. But now I'm reclaiming the territory I allowed you to take from me. I'm taking back the ground you temporarily had control over. I'm no longer playing by your rules. Because *I'm. Not. Dead.*"

I promise that if you commit to genuine change—if you begin calling out to Satan, "I'm not dead!" and take action to develop a new lifestyle—that something incredible will happen: Satan will begin to run away. And as you chase him, claiming God's promises louder and bolder, Satan will desperately flee the territory God gave you all along. It says in the Bible that if we resist the devil then he will run away from us (James 4:7), and that's exactly what will happen.

Don't forget that there's a difference between *won* and *win*. Lust may have won the moment, but it won't win the day. Insecurity may have won the day, but it won't win the week. Anger may have won the week, but it won't win the month. Pride may have won the month, but it won't win the year. Addiction may have won the year, but it won't win your life. We must continue to fight for our heart's territory. One moment, one day, one week, one month, one year at a time. You may not have won the battle, but you can still win the war.

That's the action I'm calling you to take right now. I'm calling you to make a decision to stand up, to stand firm, to take back the territory you once surrendered, and to fight for the cause of Christ.

You're not dead.

A FINAL WORD

I know it's a scary thing to watch someone faint, but beyond the medical aspect of it, you know what I find interesting? You don't realize you've fainted until you gain consciousness again. The entire time leading up to when you faint, you often know it's coming. You start to sweat, feel nauseous, and get dizzy or disoriented. But you don't remember the actual moment when you pass out. All you remember is suddenly waking up to people kneeling beside you, calling your name, asking if you're okay and handing you water. That's when you realize you had fainted.

The reason this is so intriguing to me is that it's not until you regain consciousness that you realize how *un*conscious you were. It's not until you've woken up that you realize how deep of a sleep you were in. And I think it's pretty powerful when we compare it to awakening to God's call to elevate our faith. When we come alive to the truth of God's Word and step into all that God created us to be, we will realize how dissatisfying and unfulfilling our old lifestyle was. The things that once seemed fascinating, luring, and significant will suddenly seem dull, lackluster, and petty.

We may have thought the world was blurry because blurry was our only perspective. Then we got new glasses and put on Jesus and realized there was a sharp, crystal-clear world around us the entire time. We just needed clarity to bring everything together. Once you begin to live fully awake, I promise, you'll never want to return to a sleepy lifestyle ever again.

Charles T. Studd said, "I pray that when I die, all of hell will rejoice that I am out of the fight." *That* is what it means to be a serious threat to the enemy, and that's how I want to live my life. So I'm taking this journey with you. I'm evaluating my life just like you're evaluating yours.

Let's not strive for perfection; let's strive for progression—one day, one decision at a time.

There's so much beauty ahead. It's time we choose to mount our shields, draw our swords, and pursue victory.

Let the new battle begin.

ACKNOWLEDGMENTS

A few years ago, we were hanging out with one of our best friends, Kristen. She was talking about how her grandmother was a God-fearing lady who always strived to live with a genuine and pure heart. Kristen mentioned that one time, in the midst of a conversation about living out your faith, her grandmother remarked, "But do the demons know your name?"

When Kristen mentioned her grandmother's comment, it was light-hearted and funny because you could picture an elderly little lady standing firm in her faith, calling out the "kids" like so many of our own grandparents have done themselves. But her question struck a much deeper chord with me, and I could never shake loose the idea that came with it.

So I need to start by giving a shoutout to Kristen (and likewise, "Mamaw") for birthing an idea that she had no way of knowing would take root at the time. Kristen, any impact this book makes on young adults will be a direct result of the small deposits of wisdom and truth you and Cory have poured into Megan and I throughout our friendship.

From the intense, in-depth conversations (remember the one about purpose?!) to the small, seemingly casual comments that outwardly passed unnoticed.

They've all made a difference. Thank you guys so very much.

I have to thank my wife, Megan. Y'all, I'm not easy to live with at times. Especially when I'm stressing myself out with self-imposed deadlines and getting lost in emotional thought spirals. Megan's heard it all, put up with it all, and continues to support me project after project. She prays for me, believes in me, celebrates me, and loves me something fierce. As Forrest Gump says, "Even I know that ain't something you can just find around the corner." I love you, Megan.

My family is always amazing. In particular, my dad and brother read an early draft of the manuscript and gave me some valuable feedback. The feedback was insightful and offered constructive criticism in the most gracious way. They are both writers themselves, and one of the coolest dynamics as the years have passed has been getting to support each other's projects and dreams. Thanks J-Mac and Big Al. Love you guys big. (Roll tide!)

There are three other people in particular I want to thank as well for their feedback in the early stages of this book: my former student, Natalie (who will be a best-selling author one day), my good friend, Will Scott (He writes beautiful poetry, and you need to check out his books. He's the real deal!), and our close friend and fellow teacher, Terry (a relentless prayer warrior and constant spiritual inspiration).

I also had a financial investor in the project who wishes to remain anonymous. You know who you, and when I say this book couldn't have been possible without you, I mean it! There are so many other people who have been instrumental through their prayers, support, encouragement, and love, and I'll never be able to say thank you enough.

I couldn't end this section out without thanking my cover design artist and interior formatter, Michelle Young. She is not only a precious friend but also an extremely talented author herself. All the work she did on this project—from her professionalism, to her prompt responses, to her attention to detail, to her patience, to her overall input and guidance—was of the upmost quality. Thank you for investing in this book and being intentional in the way you handled each issue addressed. I'm so incredibly grateful!

Finally, and most importantly, to the One whose name every demon knows. Thank you, Jesus, for every word you gave me and every measure of grace you offered me. This book really is all about you. You're my friend, my Father, my Savior, and my King. I love you.

NOTES

Citations

Chapter 8: "Pop-Culture"

1. "Super Bowl LIX Makes TV History With Over 127 Million Viewers." *Nielsen*, 11 Feb. 2025, https://www.nielsen.com/news-center/2025/super-bowl-lix-makes-tv-history-with-over-127-million-viewers/.

2. Talbot, Dean. "Best-Selling Book Series of All Time." *Wordsrated*, 20 July 2023, https://wordsrated.com/best-selling-book-series-of-all-time-statistics/.

3. Walsh, Shelley. "The Top 10 Social Media Sites & Platforms." *Search Engine Journal*, 7 Nov. 2025, https://www.searchenginejournal.com/social-media/social-media-platforms/.

Chapter 15: "A Lesson from Fordun"

1. Hale, Benjamin. "FREEDOM! The Real Life and Death of Sir William Wallace." *History Cooperative*, 23 Sept. 2024, https://historycooperative.org/myth-man-story-william-wallace/.

2. Hale, "FREEDOM! The Real Life and Death of Sir William Wallace."

3. Hale, "FREEDOM! The Real Life and Death of Sir William Wallace."

4. Hale, "FREEDOM! The Real Life and Death of Sir William Wallace."

5. Hale, "FREEDOM! The Real Life and Death of Sir William Wallace."

6. Hale, "FREEDOM! The Real Life and Death of Sir William Wallace."

7. Hale, "FREEDOM! The Real Life and Death of Sir William Wallace."

8. Britannica Editors. "John Of Fordun." *Encyclopedia Britannica*, 15 Mar. 2024, https://www.britannica.com/biography/John-of-Fordun.

9. James-Griffiths, Paul. "William Wallace: Scottish Freedom Fighter." *Christian Heritage Edinburgh*, 7 May 2021, https://www.christianheritageedinburgh.org.uk/2021/05/07/william-wallace-scottish-freedom-fighter/.

Conclusion

1. "Alexander the Great (356-323 BC)." *BBC News*, https://www.bbc.co.uk/history/historic_figures/alexander_th e_great.shtml.

2. "Alexander's Military Tactics." *History Archive*, https://alexander-the-great.org/warfare/alexanders-military-tactics.

3. This story is one of military and historical folklore that has been passed down through the years, the details and context varying slightly depending on the storyteller animating it. The original source or verified legitimacy of the story itself is unknown.

OTHER WORKS BY STEPHEN

TO DANCE
(Christian Fiction)

A ten-year-old boy and his grief-stricken mother journey to an alternate reality to learn how to cope with pain, make sense of tragedy, and find significance In suffering.

THE SPACE BETWEEN FIRE AND ASHES
(YA Contemporary)

Two teenagers inadvertently foil each other's plans to take their own lives and together attempt to find healing from their pain and freedom from their past.

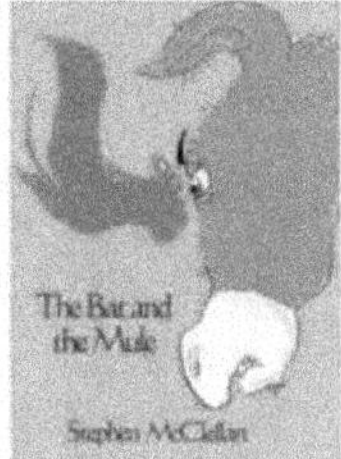

The Bath and the Mule
(Children's Literature)

Two animals with different perspectives of the world create a physical divide between each other that threatens any chance they may have at a lasting friendship.

ABOUT THE AUTHOR

Stephen McClellan is a multi-genre author who explores themes of faith, hope, loss, and love. He is passionate about instilling value into people and pursues those opportunities through helping others heal from pain and live with purpose. Wanting his influence to stretch beyond the page, his vision also includes taking a portion of the royalties he earns and reinvesting them into humanitarian organizations to support them financially and help raise awareness for their causes. If he's not reading or writing, then he's most likely pursuing life together with his wife, Megan, their son, Carson Bo, or their incredible community of friends. His family is Southern born and bred and currently lives in Tennessee.

CONNECT WITH STEPHEN:

To connect with Stephen further, find out more information about the other books he's written, or learn more about the nonprofit organizations he supports, then check out his website and social media platforms.

 https://stephenmcclellanbooks.com/

 stephen@stephenmcclellanbooks.com

 @stephenmcclellanbooks

 @stephenmcclellanbooks

www.ingramcontent.com/pod-product-compliance
Lightning Source LLC
Chambersburg PA
CBHW071733150726
47998CB00005B/1630